Unicorn Rising

Live Your Truth and Unleash Your Magic

CALISTA

HAY HOUSE

Carlsbad, California • New York City
London • Sydney • New Delhi

First published in the United Kingdom by:
Hay House UK Ltd, Astley House, 33 Notting Hill Gate, London W11 3JQ
Tel: +44 (0)20 3675 2450; Fax: +44 (0)20 3675 2451
www.hayhouse.co.uk

Published in the United States of America by:
Hay House Inc., PO Box 5100, Carlsbad, CA 92018-5100
Tel: (1) 760 431 7695 or (800) 654 5126
Fax: (1) 760 431 6948 or (800) 650 5115
www.hayhouse.com

Published in Australia by:
Hay House Australia Ltd, 18/36 Ralph St, Alexandria NSW 2015
Tel: (61) 2 9669 4299; Fax: (61) 2 9669 4144
www.hayhouse.com.au

Published in India by:
Hay House Publishers India, Muskaan Complex,
Plot No.3, B-2, Vasant Kunj, New Delhi 110 070
Tel: (91) 11 4176 1620; Fax: (91) 11 4176 1630
www.hayhouse.co.in

Text © Calista, 2018

The moral rights of the author have been asserted.

The information given in this book should not be treated as a substitute for professional medical advice; always consult a medical practitioner. Any use of information in this book is at the reader's discretion and risk. Neither the author nor the publisher can be held responsible for any loss, claim or damage arising out of the use, or misuse, of the suggestions made, the failure to take medical advice or for any material on third-party websites.

A catalogue record for this book is available from the British Library.

ISBN: 978-1-78817-091-8

Interior images: Marie-Joe Fourzali

Certified Chain of Custody
SUSTAINABLE Promoting Sustainable Forestry
FORESTRY
INITIATIVE www.sfiprogram.org
SFI-01268

SFI label applies to text stock

Unicorn Rising

unicorns are magical, beautiful, unique and confident - just like you! Happy Birthday, Jackie! ♡ Starsha

Unicorn Heart

This book is dedicated to the Love that weaves us all together. May that Love continue to rise and shine as we co-create a brighter, more magical world. And so it is.

Contents

List of Exercises
and Meditations

Introduction

If I were to ask you, 'How would you rate your life?', what would you say? Do you feel you have a good life? Or do you feel you deserve more? If you're not living in deliberate creation with your soul, aka your inner conscience, you've only scratched the surface of what life can bring. For 'embodying a divine human being', as unicorns put it, colours life like a brilliant rainbow and can make your dreams your everyday experience. And it all begins with you!

By learning how to tune in and express your Self – express your *soul* – you can find your life becoming magical. For magic isn't what you do, it's who you are. You were born with the power of Creation within you and that force never sleeps, never judges, and always loves you and holds you in the highest Light. How do you align with this grace? Unicorns are your best allies in this process. They can escort you from a 'good life' to an extraordinary existence. And this bliss doesn't have to be fleeting – it can be a consistent joy. All it takes is choosing to feel worthy enough to rise in your life and to keep soaring as you express your soul's Truth and take your life way beyond what it's been before.

Unicorn Rising

Religion, which was once our primary route into spirituality, is now falling away for many of us. Signs, symbols and synchronicities are now our touchstones for greater awareness and understanding. And what better emblem to reflect our divinity than the unicorn? Whether believed to be real or seen as an archetype of greater personal strength, unicorns are here – here to support us in creating a world where we can celebrate one another's differences, yet know wholeheartedly that we are One.

I've had the pleasure of working with unicorns for the last decade, attuning people worldwide to their consciousness through the Unicorn Healing® modality I have created. Requests for a book, plus the soaring popularity of unicorns in our everyday culture, have resulted in this guide on how to work with these graceful beings and live our best life.

Despite their fluffy, mythical persona, unicorns are master luminaries who reflect the voice of our soul – that we're the Creator incarnate, here to take consciousness to untold levels, and in the process, have fun, be free, stand strong and express ourselves without censure. Unicorns can show us our ineffable nature, which can be as soft as a flower or as powerful as a storm, and offer us the keys to unlock our life from the inside out.

What You Can Expect

We're now living in the seventh Golden Age that our planet has experienced. We entered this time, called the Aquarian Age, on 11 November 2011, and are now in a phase of ascension – the process of raising and expanding our consciousness. Each Golden Age has a theme and in this era, it's about accepting ourselves as the Creator of our own reality, both the physical life we've created and the non-physical vibrational life that's being formed through us.

As a conscious soul, you may have lived through many Golden Ages both on and off the Earth, and you will have a unique perspective and skill set. In this book, you'll learn how to live your unique path, power and purpose through releasing what's been hindering your creative sovereignty. Unicorns will be your tour guide on this adventure, for they can unveil your soul *path* (knowing and creating the life you want), your *power* (expressing your Self without censure) and your *purpose* (evolving life through your passions).

This book is both a human's guide to living as soul and a soul's guide to living as a human. You can expect to learn ways of honouring both your humanity and your divinity to live in greater harmony in the world, and woven throughout with my personal story of ascension from closed-off scientist to unstoppable She-Ra! You may find the unicorn approach to living your Truth and unleashing your magic both refreshing and original, for unicorns are masters of bringing everything back to Source and delivering wisdom in easy-to-apply ways.

Believing in Unicorns

While a soul experiences life through a physical form, their consciousness can shift from the third to the fourth and fifth dimensions. The third (3D) is when a person focuses solely on their own personal desires (aka *individual consciousness*). The fourth (4D) is when they raise their perception beyond the physical horizon and become focused on service (*group consciousness*), and the fifth (5D) is when they embody their divinity and focus on deepening their relationship with Source (*universal consciousness*). And there's a myriad of shades in between, all of which unicorns can guide us through.

Depending on our perspective, we'll sense unicorns differently. Looking through a 3D lens, we may see them as part of the fabric of myth, representing perhaps a romanticized idea of the life we could be living. From a 4D vantage point, we may see them as an archetype for our soul and its creative potential, which may make itself known through unicorn signs in our environment, dreamtime and meditative practices. And with a 5D perspective, we may recognize/remember that unicorns are real and are part of our non-physical support team, as well as evolving Source beings themselves.

It doesn't matter what 'dimensional level' you feel you're experiencing now, only that you're open to the possibility of there being more to unicorns than you already believe. Explore, experience and question. Discover who unicorns are to you. This will help you to be receptive to all they're bringing you and to all that you can do to help each other on your evolutionary paths.

How to Use This Book

Unicorns are bridges, making this is a *bridging book* for everyone to enjoy. Dimension labels are only for the benefit of the mind – ways of defining a truth that's indefinable. So please use this book in whichever way speaks to you, keeping open to new adventures along the way and to the magic that'll unfold.

Before you dive into Chapter 1, I recommend that you gift yourself with a new journal – a unicorn journal – in which you can write down what you wish to grow and transform in your life and your service to the world. Also write down any questions you have for unicorns to answer, for example 'How can I best assist you?', and any ways in which you'd like to work with them, for example 'I'd like your support with...' Writing your joint goals both sets the intention and facilitates a closer resonance and loving relationship between you and your unicorn guides.

Each chapter of *Unicorn Rising* builds upon the next, both vibrationally and in terms of how to apply unicorn wisdom in your day-to-day life. Divine wisdom and theory are grand, but if you have no experience of them, they remain outside of you. And so you'll find a vast array of exercises and meditations to help you to apply the teachings to make them your own. Your willingness to dive deep into these will help you to rise higher.

To gain the most from the teachings, I recommend you read the book in full and then reread each chapter, stopping to enjoy each exercise in sequence, keeping your journal nearby and giving yourself the space to feel and integrate what's being shared. The more time you dedicate to this process of self-healing and self-empowerment, the greater your transformation and spiritual growth will be.

Throughout the book, you'll also find self-reflective questions called #RisingReflections that ask you to pause and assimilate the teachings. Think of them as little doorways to greater understanding. Because a question unveils more magic than the answer, these are designed to help you to rise even more. (And if you love to share on social media, use the hashtag to find and interact with your fellow 'unicorners'!)

Often the journey of spiritual ascension can be overcomplicated in texts, yet it doesn't need to be. Unicorn Rising is an easy read and provides a platform for you to explore the teachings through your own experience. This is the best way to learn in our Aquarian Age – to gain wisdom through experience rather than knowledge alone. For our current age is flooded with information, yet dry on wisdom – and even more so on grounded wisdom that we can apply.

To assist you to experience unicorns, as well as your own beautiful soul, which they reflect, you'll also receive a series of attunements – energetic transmissions whereby unicorn consciousness blends with your own, creating an energetic bond that, by its very nature, is healing. Attunements support divine remembrance and help you to reclaim soul aspects, much like putting a jigsaw together, to reveal a picture of who you are and why you're here to develop. I've included two attunements in this book – the Unicorn Attunement (*see page 63*) and the Pegasus Attunement (*see page 204*) – which you can read and record to create your own guided mediations. I've also created Unicorn Healing® Meditations, an audio download of six sacred attunements, including the Unicorn and Pegasus Attunements, to bring you back to you *(see page 229)*. These meditations are embedded with musical frequencies to enhance your experience.

And so, beautiful soul, are you ready?! Fun awaits in the most magical and alchemizing of ways. Know that Creation is with you and is supporting you to rise and shine. Get ready for your best life to emerge!

And so it is. And so it is. And so it is.

She-Ra

Chapter 1
Becoming Your Own Hero

When I was five years old, my favourite toys were my She-Ra doll and her winged unicorn, Swift Wind. I wanted to be She-Ra, like many little girls, and perhaps little boys, too! Along with her unicorn, She-Ra stood for strength, purpose and the belief that everything is possible. Little did I know that someday I'd find the heroine within myself and work with unicorns to embody the same values.

As a child, nature moved through me like breath and was just as sustaining. I was often found in little nooks of the garden speaking to faeries or being charmed by conversations with stones. My gran shared my love for the Earth. Along with my mum, she taught me about the cycles of nature and how every plant had the power to heal. I loved our long walks in the country, learning about trees and the nature spirits that lived amongst them. Neither my mum nor my gran were practising Spiritualists, though other family members were, yet they both possessed a great wisdom that I admired. To this day, my gran is a soul mate, hinting from Spirit which path to take and reminding me to embody the values of compassion and kindness that she wore so well. Although she was as firm as the earth, she had a soft heart of gold. There wasn't one person who left her home without being fed. And if they weren't hungry, they'd leave with a flagon of soup!

My dad's side of the family is also intuitive, believing there's more to life than just the physical, though my dad has never featured in my life. Through years of drug use, he struggled mentally and projected his frustrations onto my mum. After a violent attack when she was six months pregnant with me, she left him for good.

Growing up, violence continued to feature in my life through fights with my sister and later through bullying at school. Like other sensitive children, I saw the world differently and so was mocked by others. To fit in, I turned my gaze away from the magic of nature and focused on being popular. As the years progressed, I became withdrawn and eventually started to self-harm and purge after eating. I learned how to conceal the effects of how I was feeling, though, and by the time I went to university I had buried much of this pain.

Throughout my honours degree in medical biotechnology, I attended services at the local Spiritualist church. The death of my gran and the prescient dreams of her clairvoyant sister, who passed soon after, convinced me there was a message waiting for me there. There was. Many times the resident medium told me I was ignoring my divine path and should be careful of the company I kept. I didn't want to listen. Being *asleep* safeguarded me from unearthing past events. It also helped to blot out the experiences of sexual abuse that followed in my early twenties. In my skewed way of thinking, if I didn't acknowledge these things, they hadn't happened.

By the age of 25, I was engaged and working in Dundee, in the east of Scotland, as a scientific researcher to create oral therapies for the treatment of cancer. Knowing that I was helping others to have a better quality of life inspired me. Yet the longer I worked in the pharmaceutical industry, the more I saw its pervasive influence on the commercialization of health. Healing can come in many forms, but this guise didn't feel right. I started to feel empty inside and wondered if doing a PhD or starting a family would replenish me. But my soul had a better idea!

Wake Up, Sleepyhead

Although I'd always wanted to be like She-Ra, at this stage of my life I certainly wasn't. Like so many others who don't believe they can be more or have more, I had *settled*. Settled in a job I didn't like, in a relationship that was stagnating, in a body that was overweight and in friendships with just my work colleagues. Nevertheless, my inner heroine was rousing herself and getting ready to slip through the bars of limitation.

Feeling weighed down by work one day, I had the urge to look up evening classes and a 10-week course in reiki jumped off the screen! Despite not knowing anything about reiki other than it claimed to heal the body using 'universal life-force energy', I signed up.

A heady blend of cynical consternation filled me as I walked into the first class. *Why am I here? How can a person 'heal' just through having hands waved over them?! This is New Age nonsense!* All those years of creating herbal remedies with my gran, believing in the power of plants to heal, had dissolved. Nevertheless, I *was* there. And something had guided me there.

My reiki teacher encouraged daily self-healing to reconcile the heaviness of my past. She felt it would reconnect me with my inner being, what she called the 'soul', the force she believed had brought me to reiki.

'The questions you have will be answered by going within,' she said.

This frustrated me, as I wanted to have everything explained to me rather than to have to explore it for myself. Yet, this advice helped me to reconnect with my soul and begin a dialogue that hasn't stopped since. I found freedom in reiki – I could breathe again! The doorway that had been open during my childhood now opened wide once again and I felt free to walk through it.

From this point on, my life changed. In my spare time, I became a reiki teacher and gave myself healing whenever I could. On busier days at work, I'd scuttle off to the bathroom to self-heal, often accompanied by the mutterings of people who thought I had a 'problem'. Well, I did spend a lot of time in the bathroom! But I didn't care.

As my awareness grew, my tolerance of those who reflected my past self waned. My belief in alternative healing was a joke to my friends – they couldn't comprehend why a scientist would believe 'energy' could heal – and so I let their closed minds sleep on. My passion for my job petered out and with it the fire for my fiancé. Although he was a caring soul, he was also an academic through and through. When I told him of my desire to leave science and become a professional healer, he tried to understand, but he just couldn't rationalize it.

The life I had created was now chaining me like the Scottish unicorn in the British coat of arms, but although I wanted to break free, my ego couldn't justify casting aside job security and a regular income. The more my ego clung to limitations, though, the worse my life got. Despite daily self-healing, the next six months saw illness after illness appear, as my body reflected my inner turmoil and attempted to get me to heed the voice of my soul. At one point, the sight completely left my right eye – body-speak for doubting the path ahead. And my body was right: I was scared; terrified of leaving all that I knew. I was stepping into a dark unknown with no hint of what was before me, only a faint voice that assured me, 'Blackness is blankness, a page waiting to be filled. Just because your life has danced to a particular tune doesn't mean you don't have the power to change its rhythm!' But although this voice was right, I still wondered who was going to pay the bills.

Apart from my mum, the gap widened between me and my family, who all expressed the opinion that being an alternative therapist wasn't a 'proper job'! Ah, how easy it can be to give our power away to our limitations and to those who reflect them. Yet, the only truth that ever serves us is the Truth of our soul.

Leap of Faith

Our soul never gives us details about what path to take, only signposts as to what is right or wrong for our overall wellbeing. I knew in my heart that leaving science was the right path for me and that the details would appear once I'd taken the leap of faith. Turning down the clamour of others' opinions allowed my inner guidance to resonate loud and clear, and I realized that those who judge are only reacting through fear – the fear that holds them back in their own lives. So

I reached a point where I no longer felt I had to be or do anything for those around me, as *their* happiness was *their* sole responsibility. It was time to let my inner She-Ra rise.

And so, after six months of self-inflicted struggle, I leaped! And oh, did it feel good! One moment I was teetering on the edge of life, appearing to have everything yet having nothing of real value, and the next I was soaring into the unknown, where yes, it appeared I had nothing, but in fact I had everything. I had faith. I had freedom. I had life. I felt the beat of my soul and the rhythm of its life flowing through me.

Time to Remember

It's incredible how quickly you become your authentic Self when you let go of what others think. Wiping their perceptions from the window of your soul allows you to see clearly, perhaps for the first time. You realize you are more than the body, the senses and the identities you have formed – you are formless, limitless and nameless. Life is no longer driven by survival: it's fuelled by exploration! The innate desire to remember and unify with all that you are awakens. You know you can have an intimate relationship with life and its creative purpose.

The way to close the gap between your finite and Infinite Self is to remember who you are. And the bridge is meditation. The world known to me as a child came alive through the stillness of meditation. It was a world of wonder, possibility and the warming glow of Spirit.

One by one, I consciously met my spirit team – the non-physical guides that assist us all to live our path consciously, power and purpose whilst in a physical body. (Every one of us has at least 11 spirit guides who reflect our creative potential.) I originally thought our spirit team consisted of those we had known from other lifetimes, but soon realized these ethereal beings could come from any dimension of Creation, and do so outside of linear time. Moreover, spirit guides aren't separate entities – they're often aspects of our own soul projected into a form that our mind can understand. Knowing our guides lends us a knowledge of our soul, which, like our spirit team, is ever-changing. There are, however, certain etheric escorts who remain with us throughout our lifetime – namely, angelic and elemental guardians.

I discovered one of my primary mentors was Archangel Raphael, the angel of trust, truth and healing. Although I didn't see him physically, I heard him through my claircognizance, the clear knowing that many people have as one of their intuitive senses. He told me my path on Earth was to be a teacher and together we would create what is now known as the Angel Healing® system with his feminine counterpart, Archeia Virtue. I hadn't heard of the term 'Archeia' before or thought that female angels existed. Eager to understand more, I asked Raphael to teach me who angels were, beyond what was already known about them.

Each day with Raphael was a page of understanding from a book that felt so familiar. I wasn't learning about angels, I was *remembering* what I already knew about them, unveiling experiences with and as the Archeia, the elementals (nature angels) and the Elohim (creator angels). My scientific peers would have had a field day with this. 'You were an angel? Oh, my God, you are so full of yourself!' Yet I found, through meditation, that my mind could be neutral and open to the possibility of more than this one existence. If the trillions of cells in our body hold the memory of all our ancestry, and in themselves are ever-changing, then it's possible that we can consciously remember all of our incarnations and not just those as a human being. When we allow ourselves to venture past the mind's intelligence to access universal intellect, we can see that we are multi-dimensional beings. Just like a rainbow, there are many different colours in our one frequency, all vibrating at the same time. This is a truth hard to see with the mind alone, yet when felt through the heart, it becomes clear.

When we open to this possibility, we can, in turn, open the door to all the incarnations our soul has, and is, living. Such lifetimes can be read in the Akashic (soul) records via meditation. From exploring my records, I came to realize that each soul originates from the same source – aka Source/the Creator/ God/Divinity – of pure love and kindness. Through creative wisdom, will and action, Source can branch out into many souls made up of the existential elements of spirit, air, fire, water and earth, and carrying within them the echo of the Creator. They pass through many planes of existence, each gathering mental and emotional capacities, energetic bodies such as the aura (light) and the *pranic* (life-force) body, and the desire to feel and sense life. They can then choose to experience different incarnations and dimensions beyond what we can discern and in as many directions as possible.

A large portion of our soul always remains in the non-physical realm as pure Source consciousness, yet when we choose to incarnate into a body, we bring a seed of Creation with us, thus beginning a journey from Love embodied to love forgotten and back again. Everything in between is our unique life experience. Or, as Victor Hugo beautifully said, 'The reduction of the universe to the compass of a single being, and the extension of a single being until it reaches God – that is love.'

The journey of descension and ascension from and back to Love explains why we all have within us a burning drive to expand life, to take it further than ever before. The extent of this drive derives from what the soul chooses as its 'earthly purpose' before incarnating.

Angels follow a similar path of creation. An angel also comes into being as embodied Love, but rarely forgets its divine heritage unless that's part of its purpose as what some would term a 'fallen angel'. In most cases, angels courier the Love of God across all realities, and do so by projecting and expressing aspects of who they are as a masculine and/ or feminine entity. (This has nothing to do with gender, but all to do with the vibration of their consciousness they are expressing at a given moment.)

If you've connected with an angel, you may have felt their presence as male or female, or a neutral blend of both vibrations. How we perceive an angel depends on what support they're giving us. For example, when my focus was learning about spiritual truths, Archangel Raphael came forward. When my goal was healing, Archeia Virtue appeared.

In most acts of healing, Virtue is the force who is assisting. Her soft pink Light helps us to heal through the freedom of forgiveness and, like all the Archeia, her feminine presence gives birth to the masculine, helping us to realize we're more than just a branch of creation, we are a Creator too, expressing Source through our physical body. And our earthly purpose, as we expand consciousness, is not to ascend some heavenly staircase, it's to bring heaven *to* Earth by embodying our divinity through our humanity, and valuing and balancing both. This is the simple yet profound Truth that our angels, guides and soul wish us to remember.

Time to Accept

It took me a while to digest everything that Raphael and Virtue shared with me. Like others who have expanded their consciousness beyond the physical horizon, I found my beliefs and identifications were challenged. I'd healed much of my past, forgiving the men who had hurt me and the girls who had bullied me at school. But I still couldn't get over knowing I'd created all my past experiences. *Rape, bulimia, self-harm – who on Earth would want to experience those awful things?* I couldn't fathom it at all! The foundation I'd known was once again breaking away, leaving me in gloopy quicksand. If it hadn't been for my incessant thirst to learn more, I would have let myself sink.

On one hand, I didn't want to sugar-coat my past by spiritualizing the experiences; they had happened and I still had the physical scars. Yet on the other hand, my soul was guiding me to broaden my perspective, to look beyond blame, judgement and pain. I had to stop reaching for wisdom with a physical stick and instead allow my consciousness to venture outside my self-created boundaries. Meditation had helped me to bridge the unseen world, but I needed help to accept myself as the creator of my reality.

I was guided to attune to other angels, to align their consciousness with my own. I wondered how I could do this, as there weren't certified angel teachers around me. Despite the angels being ever-present, I was still looking to outside sources to validate my worth.

Raphael reminded me of Dr Mikao Usui, the forefather of reiki, who had attuned himself through meditation and asked why this was any different. He was right, yet annoyingly so! Like every angel, he only ever has our best interests at heart and reflects what our soul is saying to us. Yet, his chirpy counsel to push through comfort zones often triggered an egotistic rebel in me who liked to shout: 'No, you can't make me!' Thankfully, our guides are patient.

Through attuning to other angels, I was shown ways to accept my past without carrying its ghosts in my present. (Many of those healing techniques are shared in this book.)

I was also shown how to use the Akashic records to visit other lifetimes and imprint the skills I had had in those lives on this one. Meditation journeys often led me to the star system of Sirius and the civilization of Atlantis, where I rediscovered skills in aromatherapy, crystal healing and plant medicine. Marrying this inner knowledge with a physical diploma in herbal medicine, I launched my first business, KittySoaps, making organic skincare products infused with angelic and reiki energy. In 2006, it was the first of its kind and quickly became popular.

Creating healing products every day with angels was sheer bliss! Although finances and friends were thin on the ground, my prosperity ('pro-spirit' as the angels called it) bloomed. Many of my customers felt the angelic vibrations in their soaps. They daren't use them; instead, they meditated with them and placed them by their bed to absorb the healing.

Encouraged by this, I began to connect with other nature beings – faeries, dragons and mermaids – to craft their healing soaps, too. Still relatively new to the spirit world, I had a naïve tendency to consider the beliefs of others and adopt their wisdom rather than develop my own. But my soul guided me away from learning about elementals from books and to attuning directly to them instead. The soaps also asked to be of pure consciousness, meaning my perceptions had to be clear. And so I entered every attunement with the nature beings as I did when meeting a new angel – with an open heart and mind, and a journal in hand.

As I met each elemental and wrote down how they'd like their soap to appear and what ingredients to use to reflect their being, it became apparent we'd met before, especially the faeries. Prior to awaking my consciousness through reiki, I'd thought my times with the 'little folk' were imaginary, that my younger self had made them up. However, it was my assumption of this as imaginary that was the illusion!

Even if a person chooses to be totally asleep to the world of Spirit, they have ethereal beings supporting them. In fact, every person experiencing a physical life has a guide from each of the primal elements: air, fire, water, earth and spirit. By connecting with our elemental guides and understanding the interplay of the elements within us, we can see our unique soul path, power and purpose emerge.

Over the next short while, I had the pleasure of connecting with a faery guide from the element of air, a dragon guide from the element of fire, a mermaid guide from the element of water and a crystal guide from the element of earth. As I reflected on which beings would come from the element of spirit, a soft whisper said, *'The unicorns.'*

Meeting Your Inner Hero

Unicorns guide us to meet our own soul. This is so important, for having an intimate relationship with our inner hero is the foundation for creating a magical, meaningful life. This crucial step is often bypassed in the excitement of meeting spiritual guides or encountering other incarnations, but while these adventures are fun and bring knowledge of our soul's evolution, the path of spiritual discovery is always more worthwhile if we know our roots before our branches. For Creation, in our life, in the here and now, isn't found within another person, or in some realm far away, but is animated by our very breath, in our actions, our body and soul. When we come to know this and live it every moment, *everything* becomes possible!

You may be reading this fully conscious, living unified with your inner being, or you may be a sleeping beauty just awakening. Either way, please gift yourself with the meditations and exercises that follow. Have a journal at hand to record the insights that will flow through you. To raise your energy beforehand, please drink some water, and if you're choosing to meditate at the end of your day, please rinse the back of your neck with cold water, too. The occipital ridge (where the base of your skull meets your spine) is a major point for Source consciousness to enter your body. When you feel tired or out of kilter in your mind and emotions, rinsing this point resets the nervous system and brings you back to your Self.

The following meditation takes only a few minutes to do, yet can bring about deep relaxation, self-awareness and an experience of the unconditional love that is always flowing through us. It uses something I call 'Source Breath', a sacred way of breathing that may feel familiar to you. When visiting lifetimes in Atlantis, I saw myself using this form of focused intention in empowering crystals, giving healing treatments and even imprinting my body's chemistry into plants so they yielded the best nutrition for me. We will be having fun with this breathing style throughout the book, but for now, please enjoy the meditation…

◊ Rise and Shine ◊

Meditating Unicorn

Find a comfortable place where you won't be disturbed. Sit upright with your palms facing upwards. Close your eyes and take your attention inwards and upwards to the centre of your forehead. Imagine yourself looking through this inner (third eye) point as it spirals out into Infinity.

Allow your face and body to soften. Feel the pull of gravity connecting you to the floor and Earth below.

Take three long, deep breaths. Feel your stomach expand on your inhale, and as you breathe out, draw your navel towards your spine. Decide to let go of any concerns. This is time for you, time to connect with your Self. If any thoughts appear, witness them, then turn your attention back to your breath, using the inwards and outwards flow as a touchstone to keep yourself present.

Come into your heart, sensing a bright golden flame there. Imagine its warmth and glow. Breathe into the flame – become it. Absorb its golden and white Light as you inhale and send its glow out to surround your body as you exhale.

With every Source Breath, you're raising your inner vibration and blessing your outer environment.

Breathe the golden breath down into the centre of the Earth and then up into the centre of the sun and out into all the realms of Creation.

Feel vast and aware as your Light shines from the inside out, connecting you to all life. Enjoy just 'being'.

And when you're ready to come out of the meditation, do so slowly, moving your fingers and toes as you come back into your body. Ground yourself by drinking some water and give thanks to Source.

#RisingReflections

Now it's time to get out your unicorn journal and answer the questions below. Anytime you see *#RisingReflections* in the book, it's an invitation to step through these self-reflective doorways to a greater understanding that will help you to create the positive changes you want to see in your life.

And if you love to share on social media, use the hashtag to find and interact with your fellow unicorners – it's always better to shine together!

*   *'Where can I shine more brightly in my life?'*

    'In my work, home, community, relationships, health, finances or my contribution to the world.'

*   *'What needs to change in order to raise and expand the vibration of these areas?'*

    'In my beliefs, actions, behaviour and relationships.'

◊ Me-within-Me ◊

When we're born, we have no sense of separation from anything else in our awareness. We haven't formed any identities to differentiate ourselves from our soul. But as we grow, we can become defined by our body, our personality and the beliefs through which we experience life. We may adopt the labels 'man', 'woman', 'mother', 'father', 'healer', 'teacher', 'lightworker', 'starseed', etc., but do these define who we intrinsically are? It's only when we begin to pursue a more fulfilling life that we realize that the more we label ourselves, the more we limit ourselves.

By stripping away our amassed identities, we come back to what we're always been – a divine soul having a human experience. And as we move deeper into the Truth of who we are, beyond what we can see with our eyes, hear with our ears or believe with our mind, our pursuit of a direct and united experience of our soul begins.

Through experiencing my soul, I found the courage to change my life. For the first time as an adult, it didn't feel weird to be myself! I could sense the magic that lives within the natural world, just as I had as a child, and was able to see that I was part of that glory. For, as I said earlier, magic isn't what we do, it's who we are.

In the following meditation, you're guided to meet your soul and embody yourself as a divine human being here on Earth with great magic to share. Please prepare yourself with the aforementioned 'Rise and Shine' meditation before continuing...

Feeling yourself being held in the golden Light of Source, take your attention up and through your third eye.

Imagine you're sitting in a beautiful room in front of a grand mirror. There's nothing else in the room apart from this incredibly ornate mirror.

Look at your reflection. You know your face well, but how well do you know the person behind it? Your physical body is part of Creation, loaned by the Earth to allow your soul to experience life, but it's not the real you. Affirm, 'I am more than this body,' then move deeper within.

You may not sense a reflection now, but may be feeling emotions. Feel those feelings. Emotions can define who we are at any given moment, yet they're transitory. What seems important one moment is soon forgotten. So observe your feelings. See them as waves on top of the ocean. Know that within you is an ocean of calm that never judges, simply serves you. Affirm, 'I am more than my emotions,' then move deeper within.

Beyond your body and emotions, you may find thoughts arising. Observe those thoughts. Let them wind down naturally, as if waiting for a pendulum to stop swinging. Choose to touch a deeper part of yourself. Affirm, 'I am more than these thoughts,' then move deeper within.

Beyond your body, emotions and mind lies your original Self. Invoke it now — ask it to appear in the mirror. If this is the first time you are meeting your inner being, you may see an ethereal form reflected in the mirror. This is okay. Everyone has a different experience in interpreting their soul, and usually the clarity and sense of the experience become easier to understand over time. Take time now just to be with your soul.

Ask your soul, 'Who am I?' Or another question that comes to you. Stay open and receptive, and trust that the first response you receive is your answer. Your inner being also has a gift to remind you never to be less than your magical Self. Sense this offering and receive it now.

Supported by and filled with loving consciousness, step through the mirror to merge with all that you are. Become One. Expand, radiate and make the cosmos vibrate. There is nothing you cannot be or do. Creation and Creator are now One.

Bask in this joyful bliss for as long you wish before coming out of the meditation slowly, grounding yourself with some water, stretching out your body and giving thanks to your beautiful soul.

◊   ◊   ◊   ◊

#RisingReflections

- *'The guidance and gift from my soul are significant because...'*
- *'I can be more Self-directed in my day-to-day life by...'*

Meeting the Unicorns

Chapter 2
Whole New World

O f all the elemental beings I've had the privilege of meeting, unicorns have been the most profound. And although it's been 10 years since we first met, the experience remains as vivid today as it was then.

Meeting Unicorns for the First Time

I'd sat down in my favourite meditation spot: a small corner of my living room where the sun streamed in. Although my apartment was two floors up, I could see a gorgeous silver birch tree from that spot. Its soft, diaphanous branches could have touched me if my window had been open, but it was cold outside that day and so I just admired its canopy swaying in the breeze. The more the tree moved, the more deeply I relaxed. Closing my eyes and opening my inner eye, I willed tree-like roots to grow down from my feet into the heart of Mother Earth. In my awareness, the heart of the Earth is always a ruby-red crystal that gives those who connect with it the quality of the divine feminine, plus a sense of being grounded.

Breathing the Light of this beautiful crystal, I turned my attention to the centre of the sun and then further within, to a golden orb of light that always appears in my awareness. I feel this orb represents the heart of the universe and a clear connection with my spirit team, plus the qualities of the divine masculine. Through my intentions, I brought the golden heart of the cosmos and the ruby crystal of the Earth into my heart and asked my soul to join them to complete the trinity. Then, feeling centred and ready to meet unicorns, I sent out a silent call asking for my personal guide to appear.

No sooner had the thought left me than a feeling of profound peace came in response. I felt swaddled like a newborn baby, held in sweet anticipation of a whole new world about to unfold.

In my inner vision, two unicorns approached, one male, one female, looking like huge white horses but with shimmering golden horns of light coming out of their brows. I felt exalted by their presence, yet they were easy to be around. The fragrance of their innocence filled my senses. They guided me to keep breathing deeply as they infused my consciousness. The more this attunement continued, the more clearly they manifested. Wow! Two magnificent unicorns!

They stood on either side of me and I could sense that their horns had connected to each other above my head. Turning my attention to this, I realized their combined focus created *the* most radiant rainbow. It was mesmerizing! The rainbow colours enveloped me, tender but at the same time penetrating – I was being purified from the inside out!

Directing the focus with their horns, the unicorns then touched different points on my body. They were giving me healing, but also a 'system upgrade' as each point opened like an antenna to receive their Light.

After a few minutes, the sensation subsided. The unicorns then spoke. I couldn't hear what they were saying with my physical ears, but heard it with my heart, much like a telepathic knowing. They told me about their origins, their role in creation and how they had helped humankind throughout the ages to embody its divinity.

The male unicorn, a lofty Celtic being named Hethgar, did most of the talking. He said we'd work together beyond KittySoaps to develop a special form of healing, which we have now done: Unicorn Healing®. The female unicorn held back. She didn't give a name, only the impression that she was a type of unicorn princess. Over the years, I have affectionately called her Princess, which marries well with her royal yet mischievous manner! With time, I have come to realize that the earthly names we assign to/receive from our spiritual guides aren't important; they only help our mind to understand a connection that is beyond physical intellect.

Trusting Your Connection

Despite the extraordinary attunement and healing I'd received from the unicorns, my mind was still seeking further evidence that they were real. This can happen when we connect with beings from the element of Spirit, for they vibrate at the opposite pole from more (seemingly) tangible matter. But what we seek in life will appear to us and in my case it did so in the form of a course called *Unicorn Healing Energy System©*, as channelled by Jay Burrell and Heidi Gebhard-Burger. Just days after I'd met the unicorns, a friend I'd got to know through KittySoaps shared that she was teaching this course online. I couldn't believe it and immediately signed up. We agreed on a day and time for the attunement, which was going to be delivered from a distance.

When the attunement was over, I was eager to read her feedback, as I felt there hadn't been much of a connection. Reading her reply, I burst out laughing, feeling so daft to have doubted myself and even more so to have doubted the unicorns. She wrote: 'I asked the unicorns to come forward to pass on your attunement, but they said they didn't need to. I was baffled by this and asked them for an explanation. They told me, "Calista has already attuned herself!" I hope this makes sense to you?!'

It did make sense – perfect sense! When I told her that the unicorns and I had met just days prior to her attunement, she was so happy and thrilled that she hadn't done anything wrong! At that moment, I realized no matter how far we are along our path of spiritual discovery, we're always discovering deeper depths of trust and surrender.

I apologized to Hethgar, who just smiled. He was happy I'd learned this lesson and reminded me to test him, and other spiritual guides, any time I wished. 'Discernment is as important as faith,' he said. 'Be solid in your faith. Know yourself always.'

The Origin of Unicorns

Unicorns originate from Source, just as we do. While we experience physical life on Earth, however, most unicorns experience life in celestial communities of Light. These realms exist in the Andromeda Galaxy and also within an etheric star called La-ku-ma, which is associated with Sirius, part of the Canis Major constellation. It's challenging for us to see these communities, for they vibrate in the ninth dimension of Source Light. While living an earthly life, a human being vibrates between the third and fifth dimensions, meaning it's only possible for us to visit these celestial realms by expanding our consciousness. This can be achieved through meditating with our unicorn guides and asking them to support the alignment of our vibration to that of their realm for a while.

The cosmic dwellings of unicorns are devoid of the lower frequencies of fear, judgement and separation. The communities they live in are formed through their co-operation with the other beings that live there, all woven together in unity consciousness and love for all. When you visit these realms, expect to hear the most incredible music! Unicorns love music and the joy it brings. They also value fun, dance, play and nature. There are fields upon fields of fragrant flowers in La-ku-ma, in the most extraordinary gold, rainbow and diamond-like colours.

There are many different species of unicorn, and different lineages are evolving in dimensions both within and beyond our universe. There are royal lines of unicorns, many of which are evolving alongside the angelic kingdom, supporting the Archangels and Archeia, as well as the Elohim, who oversee the unicorn, elemental, devic and inner-Earth communities. There are also species of unicorns specifically concerned with developing the civilizations of Atlantis and Lemuria. (If you remember these times, you may recall that unicorns took physical form then, as did elementals – something that may return if we learn to cohabit harmoniously with all species on/in Mother Earth.)

The unicorns who are specifically focused on helping the soul of the planet, Gaia, to ascend have elemental, *Sidhe* (ancient faery) and Celtic ancestries, and have many etheric retreats all over the world. If you encounter a silver birch or copper beech tree, you may sense the presence of these unicorns, for they are attracted to the frequency of these trees. Throughout the writing of this book, I was drawn to walk by these trees and was reminded that the more we breathe in their energy, the more we attune to these types of unicorn.

What Do Unicorns Look Like?

When unicorns take a physical form, they appear as white horses and their purity makes them glow. Their luminescence is due to the frequency of light they are vibrating at, which, like their heavenly homes, is the ninth dimension of Source Light, though their consciousness can be vaster than this, and beyond what we class as 'dimensional'. From a dimensional perspective, we could say that most of humankind is living at the density that is furthest from Source (3D reality), where the focus of life is material-based only. Because you're reading this book, your awareness will have lifted to that of the unseen world and will be anchored in a 4D or 5D frequency. As your consciousness has evolved, you may have noticed that you have started to look younger and feel lighter, perhaps appearing to *glow* in your photographs. Expanding your consciousness really is the best, and cheapest, beauty aid! As the unicorns say, 'As we grow, we glow!' I wholeheartedly agree – I've never looked, or felt, younger than I have since working with unicorns!

As well as glowing, the body and mane of a unicorn can change colour. Although Hethgar comes forward with a white body and golden mane, he has changed colour when I've been working with clients, depending on what their healing intentions have been.

All unicorns, however, as their name suggests, have a single spiralling horn coming from their third eye – the energy centre (chakra) of enlightenment, intuitive sight and wisdom. This horn isn't physical, it's vibrant Source energy that spirals Light out into Infinity and back again. The Light creates a focused vortex that can hold, emit and transmute energy like a crystal wand. The horn itself is often sensed as silver, white or gold. As a unicorn develops its consciousness, the radiance of its horn changes from white to golden white to deep gold and in some cases to a translucent diamond-like Light.

Although a unicorn's horn may appear to be a phallic symbol, its vibration is that of the divine feminine too, for it is equally giving and receiving, and symbolizes the Infinite wisdom of the unicorn race. During your attunement to unicorns (see page 63), you'll receive your own etheric unicorn horns. These will be placed in your third eye, heart and palm chakras to ignite your own divine magic.

Whenever a unicorn horn is directed with intention, pure Source consciousness is delivered to that area through a varied spectrum of colour rays, as you'll discover when working with unicorn healing energy.

As your awareness expands, you may come to perceive unicorns as formless beings, for your consciousness will be blended with theirs. I rarely see Hethgar and Princess as separate entities now, yet on days when I've felt in need of a little boost, they've appeared by my side.

Why Unicorns are Returning to Our Awareness

Unicorns have existed since the dawn of Creation, but they come into our awareness at pivotal times of ascension, i.e.

when humanity is ready to break through old paradigms and raise its collective consciousness. On 11 November 2011, we entered such a Golden Age: the Age of Aquarius, a 2,000-year cycle that mirrors our desire to live fully and freely as one united race.

Although unicorns are synonymous with sugary fairytales, they are far from *fluffy*! As masters of Spirit, they're our greatest allies in managing shifts in consciousness, for as soon as we invite them into our life, we invite in our soul.

Do you see unicorns everywhere? If you do, it's an indication that you're raising your vibration to the level on which you want to live your life. You may have felt their loving presence in your dreams or meditations, or perhaps you see them around you in branding, clothing and across social media. Have you noticed the soaring popularity of colouring books? And the Infinite choice of hair colours now available? The rainbow light of the unicorns is flowing through our modern culture with the motto 'Colour me and my world differently.' The desire to express our inner unicorn is flowing through us each day and this 'unicorn wave' doesn't show any sign of stopping! For many awakened souls are ready to embrace the new Golden Age and create a world where we can celebrate one another's differences yet know in our heart that we are One, a world where humanity can be our race and love our religion.

If you lived during the Flower Power movement of the late 1960s, you may remember unicorns appearing in the campaigns for peace. Going further back, they emerged in a series of seven medieval tapestries – the most stunning and intricate works of art to survive from the late Middle Ages. These hangings can be seen in the Cloisters section of the Metropolitan Museum of Art in New York, and depict both the coveted and hunted nature of unicorns. Greek natural history, Indian and Chinese cultures, and both the Old and New Testaments also cite the holy aspect of unicorns. In the allegoric text *Physiologus*, written in the 2nd century AD, the unicorn allows itself to be captured only by a virgin girl. This could symbolize the story of the baby Jesus growing in the Virgin Mary's womb or, in a more current sense, that embodying the purity of our soul releases our innate wisdom.

I believe that unicorns – like the concepts of Christ Consciousness and the Holy Grail – help us to uncover the secret of life: that we are our *own* Creator. They help us to see that it's safe to stand out from the crowd and, in doing so, inspire others to do the same. This freedom of being is power – the power that was suppressed in the last Piscean Age and a force that many who are still focused on the 3D world would also like shadowed. For standing in your power brings responsibility, which, if you aren't ready to embrace it, feels more of a burden than a liberty.

In art, literature and even nursery rhymes, unicorns have been hunted and caged. In heraldry, like the royal coat of arms for Scotland, unicorns wear collars and are kept chained. As a Scot, I could believe this represents how those in authority control the masses. Beyond cultural identification, I see the unicorn representing our capacity to break free of anything that binds. For in our Aquarian Age, we're realizing that we're both the clay and the hands that mould it. And although we can feel stifled by our government, and even more by those around us, freedom of being is always our choice. I spent years feeling locked in my own life, immobilized in relationships and held captive by the demons of my past, until the unicorns showed me that by following the voice of my soul, I could break free. They reminded me, that I – just like you, beautiful soul – had a force within, greater than any challenge, and a light brighter than any darkness that had been created. And if I trusted that Creation was cheering for me every moment, I could work miracles.

Unicorn Gifts for Humanity

Whether you believe unicorns are an archetype of greater possibilities or see them as real beings is of no consequence. They believe in you and the greatness that lives within you. If unicorn signs are prevalent in your awareness, know it's a calling card from your soul to experience deeper levels of freedom, joy, play and love in your life, and to alight from fear. For eons, humanity has picked up and perpetuated fear-based behaviour and beliefs, and with them the sense of having to force life to happen. Unicorns, being fearless, completely trust in Source and therefore live by Divine Will. As such, they offer us ways to master our mind and emotions, so we can surrender any control tendencies and instead follow our joy, for in the state of joy all emerges with perfect grace.

It's been written in other spiritual books that unicorns only work with virtuous human beings. This is not true. Unicorns are not judgemental and are accessible to any person who genuinely asks for their support. As human beings, we all have free will and with it the power to choose our reality from moment to moment. For this reason, unicorns can't impose their assistance on us without our consent. But when they are called in, they delight in helping us to discover our unique path, power and purpose, and then, with joy, to express this in the world.

Freedom of Expression

Similarly, unicorns never assume that humanity needs 'healing'. They only see us as our highest Selves, always aligned to that which we are. Nonetheless, they understand that living a physical life with free will can bring conditioning and challenges that separate us from our true Selves. This separation can in turn make us feel immobilized and cause a build-up of resistance and dis-ease to manifest in our body. Unicorns support us in unearthing the root cause of dis-ease so we can move forward with our lives. Their healing energy, when given, is always received first by our soul and is then directed to where it is needed to balance us, whether on a mental, emotional and/or physical level. As unicorns are masters of the element of Spirit, their vibration contains the combined wisdom of the elemental and spiritual realms. This means they can assist with any healing intention. Whether we want to revitalize our finances, career or health, or to give and receive greater love, fun and clarity, they can assist us.

From witnessing Unicorn Healing® sessions over the last decade, I have learned that our celestial friends help us by giving us the energetic virtues they carry in their consciousness. We can merge with these and also allow them to develop within us like a seed growing and maturing over time. When you attune to unicorns in the next chapter, you'll receive the following virtues and any others specific to your divine path:

• appreciation

• compassion

• confidence

• faith

• grace

- innocence

- joy

- love

- majesty

- purity

- self-belief

- trust

- unity

- wisdom

By receiving these gifts, you'll become your noble Self and therefore a template of nobility for others.

You'll also find that receiving their energy can support:

- accepting your noble Self – believing Source lives within you, as you

- awakening and embodying your soul's gifts and earthly purpose

- balancing and expanding the consciousness of your being

- bridging the multi-dimensional realms of Creation

- clearing old beliefs and programmes to reveal the root cause of dis-ease

- encouraging fun – redefining 'work' as 'play'

- feeling connected to all life – embodying unity consciousness

- harmonizing and strengthening your relationships, especially your soul connection

- healing ancestral/childhood/inner-child issues, as well as the effects of trauma

- inspiring self-belief – instilling the faith and courage to move out of your comfort zone

- overcoming addiction, fear and self-limiting patterns

- releasing pent-up emotions, including feelings of being overwhelmed by the need to 'keep up' with life

- removing unhealthy attachments and creating boundaries where needed

- strengthening creativity

- witnessing the blessings and beauty in all

As you move forward with your unicorn guides, you'll find more ways to draw on their Light in order to bring about the changes you're ready to see in your life.

Does Everyone Have a Unicorn Guide?

Yes! Every human being has a unicorn guide under their spiritual umbrella of care. As you journey through this book, you'll come to know your own guide and enjoy many wonderful adventures together!

Your unicorn guide reflects your soul. They are a facet of you and you of them. Because of this, when you first consciously meet each other, you may recognize them as a familiar friend. When I look at Hethgar and Princess, I see facets of myself – the shiny parts! For unicorns hold up a mirror in which you see your most radiant Self – the you that's beyond any limitations, as you discovered in the 'Me-within-Me' meditation (*see page 18*).

In our Aquarian Age, we no longer learn through the mind alone – that's simply not enough to quench the thirst of our soul. Instead, we understand universal truths through experiencing them. So it's only through *experiencing* the presence of your unicorn guides that you'll really get to know them.

What might they be like? Unicorns, like angels, can manifest as masculine or feminine consciousness or a blend of both. So you may sense, as I did, that two individual unicorns are presenting themselves as your guides, one male and one female. And when you invoke one guide, you may feel the presence of the other as well. For example, Hethgar always comes forward as my main unicorn guide, yet Princess is always there, albeit in the background. Others in my spirit team are predominantly male in their vibration, too. My soul assigned these guides to me to help heal the wounds I was carrying from the masculine influences in my life. For our soul always selects the best spiritual teachers for our earthly life, whether they be male or female in vibration, physical or etheric in form, and whether their relationship with us brings balance on a micro or macro scale.

Over the years, I've come to realize our unicorn guides match our individual soul ancestry and the gifts we're here to share. For example, if you're among the many who resonate with being a 'starseed' – someone who believes they originate from another star system, dimension and/or planet – you'll invariably connect with galactic unicorns. And you may communicate through light-language – a universal way of exchanging using energetic patterns, sounds and colour frequencies – as opposed to using a more linguistic exchange if you have a different ancestry.

In appearance, though most unicorns are white, many Unicorn Healing® students have unicorn guides that manifest in their awareness with a brown or black body. This doesn't signify anything sinister – far from it! Their guides appear like this to lend them support in integrating their inner shadows and exploring their deeper roots.

Similarly, some people perceive their unicorn guides as baby unicorns and as they evolve together, their form changes into that of a fully-grown unicorn. Having 'younger' guides is a reminder to meet unicorns – and the seen/unseen world each day – in the state of knowing nothing, of being innocent like a child, so life can make an impression on us. When we open to Spirit like this, we can *listen* more carefully and receive the wisdom that not only serves us, but also the creation of a brighter world.

Both angels and unicorns support us in embodying our loving Truth. While angels open the doorway to our spirituality via our heart centre, unicorns usher us through by connecting us to our soul and showing us our creative potential. They inspire us to raise our standards in every area of our life – never to settle for less than we are.

See your unicorn guides as personal soul coaches who forever have your back! Let them assist you in keeping your intentions high and clear, and having the courage, dignity and faith to live your best life. Lean into them for guidance as to what your path and purpose are, and absorb their strength to stand tall in your power. They can support you as you manifest your dreams, but you must call them in first.

◊ Calling in Your Unicorns ◊

The call to your unicorns doesn't need to be a long-winded prayer or invocation – a simple silent request is all that's needed to receive their help.

Then relax and stay open to the many ways in which your guides will answer you: directly through telepathic and/or light-language communication, or indirectly through signs and symbols in your environment, or through visitations in your meditations, healing practices and dreamtime. Their insights may also come to you via another person, or a song you hear or even spontaneously compose. Listen and be receptive, for your unicorn guides are always with you and love you beyond measure.

As they gather to meet you:

◊   Ask yourself, 'Do I have any resistance to meeting my unicorn guides? Do I feel worthy of experiencing their love?'

◊   Take a few minutes to witness the answers and feelings that arise.

◊   Decide to let go of everything that might limit your connection by affirming aloud:

> *'Loving Source, please remove on all levels of being [the resistance/any limiting beliefs] to fully opening to the Light of unicorns and the Light of my soul. I release these now and reclaim my power, trusting I am worthy, supported and loved.*
>
> *Thank you. And so it is.'*

◊   Surrender all limitations to Source, as well as any preconceptions about what unicorns are. Meet them with an open perspective so they can make an impression on you and so you can best enjoy each other's loving company.

Please prepare yourself with the 'Rise and Shine' meditation (*see page 16*) before continuing...

◊   ◊   ◊   ◊

◊ Meeting Your Unicorn Guide ◊

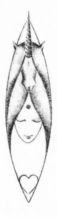

Unicorn Guide

*Feeling yourself being held in the golden Light of Source,
take your attention up and through your third eye.*

*Imagine you're in a beautiful forest comprised of your
favourite trees, flowers and animals. Take a moment to
fill your senses with the fragrances, colours and warm
sunlight. There's nothing for you to do other than just be...*

*Sit down on the mossy forest floor. The uplifting music
of faeries begins to enfold you, raising your vibration and
signalling that unicorns are near. Send out a heart call to
meet your personal unicorn guide now.*

*Open your senses as one, two or more unicorns approach.
Welcome them by bowing and then ask for your main
unicorn guide to step forward. Look into their eyes, feeling
the Light of your soul and theirs blending together.*

Breathing in their presence, open to what is sacred about your connection. Have you experienced other lifetimes together?

Take time to get to know them. Do they feel male, female or of a neutral vibration? Are they old or young? What is the colour of their body, mane and horn? Ask if they've a name and how you can serve each other, trusting always that the first response that comes to you is your answer.

Share any concerns or questions you have with your unicorn guide, especially if the guidance you seek concerns your soul path and purpose. If it feels right, ask them to send healing to specific areas of your life. Relax as you receive this loving Light, breathing out the old and breathing in the new.

Bask in the bliss of being with your unicorn guide, sharing and exchanging what feels right.

And then come out of meditation slowly, grounding yourself with some water and stretching out your body.

#RisingReflections

- *'Meeting my unicorn guide is significant because...'*
- *'Accepting their love, healing and wisdom has enabled me to...'*
- *'I'll call in my unicorn guide to support me with... and I can support them by...'*

Unification

Chapter 3
Attuning to Your Self

Wanting to know and explore our divine path drives us to seek a better way to live, a better way to be. Each one of us has at some point been spiritually shipwrecked – stranded on our own discord. And although these moments can feel disabling, they're our most creative times. From breakdowns, breakthroughs blossom and they can inspire us to live our dreams when we follow the Light of our soul.

After meeting and attuning to the unicorns, I felt a deeper pull to turn to the subtlety of my soul to direct my choices. And the more I leaned in to listen, the clearer everything became. My mind still wittered on about the risks of 'this' and the neurosis of 'that', but a deeper voice also emerged and it felt so steady. I realized this was the voice of my soul, the voice that had nudged me to study reiki, to leave science and to begin a new adventure alongside Spirit. Each time I invoked the unicorns to co-create their soaps, I sat with Hethgar afterwards to learn more about my instinctive Self, for his presence naturally amplified my intuition.

Making energy-infused skincare came so naturally to me, as did knowing how to blend the essential oils to best mimic the vibration of the beings represented. For example, to capture the essence of a unicorn, I merged the earthy tones of sandalwood, lavender and patchouli with uplifting citrus oils – a fusion that transported me and my customers into *the* most magical forest! I'd never taken a course in aromatherapy, so *why* did it feel so instinctual? Through meditating, I saw myself as an aromatherapist in Atlantis and wondered if the skills of one lifetime could transfer into another. I turned to Hethgar for an explanation…

Awakening to Your Life Movie

My first awareness of Atlantis was when I was a young girl. My mum had several books on the subject, which suggested Atlantis was an ancient civilization as advanced technologically as it was spiritually that now lay buried under the Atlantic Ocean. From meeting angels and exploring the era of Atlantis with Hethgar, I've come to understand Atlantis to be much, much more!

Awareness of this civilization seems to act as a 'trigger' within our cellular make-up, helping us to awaken spiritually from the inside out. Perhaps you are drawn to Atlantis, too. Or maybe your parents were. As every generation evolves, what our parents understood through book learning, we can experience wholly through our awareness.

According to Hethgar, the 'memory' of Atlantis emerges when we are ready to expand our consciousness. He maintains this is facilitated by the fact that all human beings currently living on Earth have lived an Atlantean life, if not many lives. And contrary to the idea of Atlantis having existed, from a linear perspective, for 1 million years before its conclusion around 13,000 BCE, it still exists to this day and evolves through us all. A truth that is challenging to grasp with the mind but, when allowed to sit in the heart, flows freely...

Perhaps like me, your soul decided to return to Earth to support the birth of our new Golden Age, using the conscious awareness of the last ascended age, which many feel was/is the time of Atlantis. You may also have brought in remembrance of ascended ages from other star systems, like Sirius, especially if you are here to support humanity to rise. If you have goosebumps – I call them 'truth bumps' – sensing the certainty of this, consider that your love of spirituality, the healing arts and empowerment are rooted in your divine path. Often, what we're naturally drawn towards is what we have lived before or will to come. The reason for this is to bolster our soul to express its inherent purpose – to expand life, to take it beyond where it's been before.

Before incarnating into physical form, our soul will have decided on an area (or areas) to develop during its sojourn on Earth. Because the soul has a neutral perspective, it appreciates the value in every life experience, whether that's to grow through adversity or privilege, poverty or wealth, health or dis-ease, and all the myriad of shades in between. Many souls, while naturally expanding life, do so with the added awareness of living their divinity. This remembrance of Self comes to all souls participating in a Golden Age. Therefore, you may easily sense times in Atlantis (among other times and dimensions) and imprint the wisdom that best meets your desire for expansion in this Golden Age. It's all part of the 'deluxe upgrade' in choosing to live consciously.

I liken life experience to a cosmic cinema with Infinite screens (possible realities) and Infinite movies (possible lifetimes within those realities). Upon deciding to incarnate, our soul lines up at a chosen cinema and then picks the movie it wants to enjoy, whether an action adventure, drama, rom-com... sci-fi thriller, even! And if we don't like what we see, we can switch screens to enjoy something else. For we always have the power to change our life experience.

Awareness of our own 'life movie' is rekindled when we invite unicorns into our life. Without holding back, they enable us to see that we're either resisting transforming our reality through the fear of taking personal responsibility or have decided to move freely into a new adventure, empowered through following the voice of our soul.

And, just as when going to the cinema we may take along our favourite foods and friends, so our inner being decides upon the skills and relationships that'll best serve in that particular life. For example, my soul brought along aromatherapy skills and contact with specific Spirit guides to support the set-up of KittySoaps. This natural process of our soul's expansion transcends the Law of Attraction, which is a spiritual decree of our manifested (time and space) universe that returns to our knowing when we become consciously aware and states that whatever we focus on we attract, and follows the Law of Creation, a spiritual decree that exists beyond manifested reality, which returns to our knowing when we accept we are the Creator, experiencing life as we craft it.

Awakening Your Potential

From our soul's perspective, all realities connect and flow through the moment we're experiencing. And so the most rewarding way to enjoy life is simply to be here *now* – to feel the dance of life moving through us as we watch it express itself around us. Having an awareness of other lifetimes, like ones in Atlantis, is useful, but if we're not careful, it can entertain us more than empower us! I have seen many people (including myself) identify with characters from other lifetimes and relive and value these existences over their current life. Does this sound familiar? I feel many of us, as intrepid seekers, walk through this shadowed valley of self-limitation to gain a greater perspective on who we are. But then, as attachments to other existences fade from view, we no longer feel confused about what our divine path is, for we come to understand we're always on the path, *as the* path itself!

So, although it was important for me to know about Atlantis when later creating the Atlantean Crystal Healing™ modality, I decided with all my being to focus solely on the now. With this freedom came the realization that my soul, through the Law of Creation, could bring in any skills that best served my path, without other-life exploration.

I quickly put this theory into practice, nudged by Hethgar to leave out 'analytic reasoning'! As a scientist, I was taught to trust in a world that I could see with my eyes; now I had to trust in what couldn't be seen, only felt within my being and mirrored as my reality. After many tag-team battles of 'logic vs truth'/'ego vs heart', I became a believer in the divine creativity that we're all born with.

Sometimes I asked for the knowing of a skill to be uploaded into my awareness and other times for the imprinting of an energetic quality, like forgiveness. The more I opened to this process, the more I saw these energies weren't coming from something outside myself, but their potential was being activated within me. Unicorns say that because all souls are an extension of Source, they all have the 'template' of Source's creative potential – meaning that everything becomes consciously possible when we trust in the Law of Creation!

Believing in this reality has given rise to so much magic in my life and I'm seeing the same for you too, beautiful soul. Please enjoy this extraordinary exercise to activate and further your creative potential...

◊ Awakening Your Potential ◊

◊ Prepare yourself with the 'Rise and Shine' meditation (*see page 16*).

◊ Then, feeling yourself being held in the golden Light of Source, take your attention up and through your third eye.

◊ Imagine a lift in front of you and step inside. As the door closes, press the button marked 'Heart'.

◊ Sense yourself moving downwards until you've arrived at your heart.

◊ Exit the lift and move into the deepest expanse of your Self. For a moment, imagine you are a child in a sweet shop, only instead of sweets, there before you is every personal quality that you could ever want.

◊ Feeling grateful, ask yourself, 'What would best support me in my life and bring me joy right now?'

◊ And then affirm aloud:

> *'Loving Source, please activate within me [the qualities that came to your awareness] in direct accordance with my soul's path and purpose.*
>
> *Thank you. And so it is.'*

◊ Breathe in all of the qualities you wish to call in/allow to activate... Let them become part of you.

◊ Witness everything that switches on. There's nothing for you to do or imagine here. Just continue to breathe deeply as you allow this energetic activation to take place.

◊ Trust in the simplicity of this process as you believe in your creative capabilities. Accepting your divine potential is the greatest gift you will ever give yourself and by living this grace, you illuminate this capability for others to enjoy.

◊ When you are ready to close the space, give thanks for all that was switched on.

Repeat this activation whenever you're guided to do so.

◊   ◊   ◊   ◊

#RisingReflections

- *'The gifts my soul called in were...'*
- *'These will enhance my life by instilling greater joy and...'*

Choosing to Live Your Path

Accepting that your soul and inherent gifts are Infinite is one thing, but living daily the ineffable Light of who you are is by far another! To embody this grace, it's crucial to discern the voice of your soul so you can trust its unconditional direction over the voice of your ego, which only gives a conditional idea of who you are. For there is a world of difference between wanting to know and live your path, and making the decision to personify it. Remember, your personal power is always derived from the choice to be your true Self – a decision you make with your heart to live fully, surrendering yourself to the Light of your soul and letting the outcome of this covenant land where it may. This is the noble path that unicorns walk and their highest vision is for humanity to walk it, too.

When I first learned this via Hethgar, it made sense, yet triggered so many questions, too. My mind had a field day trying to process it all. *So, I am supposed to just listen to my inner guidance and follow its direction – is that right? How will I know this direction is the best course of action? What if the voice of my ego is too loud? What if I am steered off my path?* My mind brought up so much resistance, yet Hethgar remained steadfast and assured me:

> *You'll know when your soul speaks to you, for the voice will be clear and direct, and will give you a sense of expansion as it replies to your query. You'll know when you are following the voice of your soul, for you'll experience a life of happiness. And although challenges may arise, you'll recognize them as opportunities to grow and thus respond to them through inner enquiry rather than reacting outwardly.*
>
> *You'll know when your ego speaks to you, for the voice will be critical and give you a sense of*

contraction as it replies to your query. You'll know when you are following the voice of your ego, for you'll be preoccupied with attaining personal desires, and you'll experience life with self-doubt and fear.

Know the soul only speaks of right and wrong, and only seeks expansion through the joy of being. It never defends itself or judges you. For your soul is fearless and unbounded, and loves you eternally. Your soul is the core of your conscience, loves and personality, and aligns you with Source when you listen and follow its way. Trusting your divinity is trusting life itself. Trust your soul. Follow its path of joy and know that all of Creation is with you.

There is nothing like a dose of divine certainty from a huge Celtic unicorn to get you moving! Fuelled up, I made the choice, there and then, to follow the voice of my soul and surrender to living my path, come what may. I still wasn't sure what 'my path' was, other than it involved teaching and that it was constantly being created through my choices, but I was sure I would find out.

Letting Life Flow through You, As You

After a few months of building my business from home, spending spare time in meditation with unicorns and angels and slowly deciphering the voice of my soul, I was inspired to sell my skincare at local mind, body, spirit (MBS) fairs. I felt the same sense of home entering this world as I had when studying reiki. It was refreshing to make new friends, especially those who shared my love of Spirit, which in this reality was everyone.

From MBS fairs, Hethgar nudged me to share KittySoaps at my local farmers' market. (Our unicorn guides really do nudge us to take inspired action, especially if we're not paying attention!) So one Saturday morning I went to do a recce of the market and saw a trader selling soap. When I told him I'd been drawn to sell my soaps there, he didn't look pleased to hear it. But I didn't think anything of it and decided to apply for a stall. Within a few weeks, I'd received a call from the council lady who oversaw the approval of stall applications. She asked me if my products were safety tested and I told her I'd done my own assessment, thinking that would be okay given my scientific background. Unsure whether this was sufficient, she appointed a trading standards officer to come and inspect my home and manufacturing procedures. I later discovered that the soap trader I'd met had complained my soaps weren't 'certified' and said that selling them at the market would be 'against the law'.

After a few hours of scrutinizing my safety measures and soap manufacture, the trading standards officer said everything was perfect in his eyes, but in the eyes of the law, each of my products needed independent safety testing. Owing to the number of products I had, having each one assessed would have bankrupted me. My heart sank. I'd put everything into KittySoaps. Waking up each day to make these gorgeous products was so much fun. And it felt so safe and comfy in my kitchen. Now, that old familiar sense of teetering on a tipping point was swirling through my body like an icy breeze.

Seeing the shock on my face, the trading standards officer was sympathetic. He was a nice guy who, after all, was just doing his job. As he left my flat, he said, 'Have you heard about the local competition to win a shop? Why not open a therapy centre and save up to get your products safety tested?'

I could have kissed him! Was this the next part of my path? Did I have what it would take? 'Of course you do,' the voice of my soul assured me.

Trusting the Signs

The next day, I had a meeting with the council lady to discuss how my visit with trading standards had gone. She was sorry to hear my business had to close, but although I appreciated her kindness, the butterflies in my tummy were taking up all my focus!

I asked for more information about the shop competition and she explained that entrepreneurs could pitch their business ideas to a panel of investors. The winning prize was one of three shop units in a local shopping centre, along with marketing support and free rent for the first year. It sounded too good to be true!

When I asked her for an application form, she said I'd better be quick in completing it, as the closing date was just two days away! *What?!*

'It's okay,' my inner voice comforted. 'Just take the application form and fill it in.'

And so that is what I did and, beautiful soul, I can tell you I put everything into that application – into my vision for a holistic centre that sold healing gifts, crystals and skincare, and offered therapies, talks and classes to help the community to trust in their divinity, too. I often visited the empty shop units, first deciding which one was best for my centre and then visualizing it as a thriving business. I'm sure the shopping centre's security staff thought I was weird, as I'd linger outside the space, imprinting on it my sense of talking to customers, giving treatments and teaching workshops. But by imagining the centre as already manifested, I was creating that reality. And, as ever, when we are allowing something that feels soul-led to come into form, there was a centred sense of joy and expansion blended with a clear knowing that this was the *right* path. The unicorns also made sure I saw their many physical signs that confirmed the guidance of my soul.

After being shortlisted, I was asked to present my idea to the panel of investors who would decide on the winner. Despite trusting that this was meant to be, I was *so* nervous. My ego ranked these executives higher than me and showcased many scenarios of them ridiculing me and my vision of being a spiritual teacher. But as I gathered myself together to walk to the presentation, I saw a statue of a unicorn and felt Hethgar saying, 'I am with you.' And then, walking through the front doors of the shopping centre, I felt drawn to look up and right overhead was the word 'unicorn'! And as if this wasn't enough to ease my nerves, I discovered the panel of investors had arranged themselves in the very shop unit that I'd envisaged as my store. So I took a deep breath and gave the presentation my all. Some of the panel members did give me funny looks when I referenced 'angels' and 'unicorns', but by then I was back in my centre and hopefully in my soon-to-be holistic centre, too.

The evening before hearing the final news about the competition, my ex-fiancé and I went to the beach. I was so grateful for his cheery company, for all the while the competition had been running, my current romantic relationship had been coming to an end. And although I felt I *should* be concerned about that, all I experienced that night was the support of my best friend and the palpable cushion of Spirit around me. I have never felt so *held* by the love of Creation as I did at that moment. It felt as though I were being embraced within and without, ensuring that Ethereal Light – the name the unicorns had suggested for my store – had to manifest. I couldn't think just one negative thought, for it was crucial to stay in the vibration of trust for what was coming next. And this was reflected in the sky that evening. Oh, how I wish I had a picture to show you, for there were so many unicorn-like clouds and symbols of wings cast over the horizon! My vision was appearing right before my eyes and manifested fully the next day when an investor called to say I had won! And not only that, but the panel had also decided to give me the shop unit from my vision.

What a whirlwind! First creating a soap business, then losing that business, followed by winning a competition that gave me the resources for my dream holistic centre! And despite having no money for shop displays and stock, I soon found those resources appeared too, and within three weeks Ethereal Light was open. It opened, in fact, on 31 October 2009, the time of the Celtic New Year, which I had chosen to honour Hethgar for all his help. He had been ever-present, providing me with a steady stream of signs, symbols and synchronicities to keep me certain in uncertain times and prompting me that no matter what the odds, dreams can come true when we choose to live in trust and follow our joy.

Superhero Add-ons

So I learned that if we trust the guidance of our soul, miracles manifest. And my faith in my inner being was further increased through attuning to the ethereal beings of Creation. Over the years, I've attuned myself to unicorns, angels, nature spirits, crystals, sacred geometry, the wisdom of civilizations – really, whatever my soul has guided me to. It took me a while to trust in the process, but all became easier once I got out of my own way.

As I made these sacred energetic connections and merged my consciousness with theirs, I felt pieces of my soul coming back together. Like the 'Awakening Your Potential' exercise (page 51), this form of 'soul retrieval' activates aspects of ourselves that we may not have been consciously aware of or brings back parts of us that have felt missing or lost. Attunements are a way of using our intention to unite our humanity with our divinity. They help us to understand ourselves better, while fortifying us with an array of superhero add-ons.

As I allowed more of myself to become awakened, I wanted to share the gifts that were coming through me with my Ethereal Light clients. It felt so natural to hold the space for them to meet and merge with similar qualities, so they could enjoy a more intimate relationship with their soul and its gifts. It lit me up seeing them positively transform during the attunements and hearing about all the encouraging shifts that happened afterwards. I came to realize that the joys we hold dear in life are, in truth, our soul's gifts and that our passions fuel our purpose.

And so I – really, we, with the consent of your soul and unicorn guides – would like to attune you to the collective consciousness of the unicorn realm, so you're forever linked to unicorns and can channel their Light for the benefit of all concerned. This unconditional gift is given to strengthen your connection with your unicorn guides and to increase your faith in yourself. From witnessing the extraordinary rise in vibration of those who've received the following unicorn attunement, I can say I'm hopeful you'll feel as held by Creation as they were and that from that loving certainty you'll live your Truth with greater ease.

Attuning to Unicorns

Although this is a very magical experience, it is also a very grounding one. There's nothing to fear if you've never received an attunement before, for it's always given at a soul level, meaning you'll receive it in the best possible way for you. The unicorns always deliver healing before attuning you to their Light. Receiving healing first alleviates any sudden shifts in your vibration from detoxifying your system and energetic bodies. Then any blocks that may be hindering you in your life can leave you safely and easily. But the way you receive and process this healing is self-directed, which means if you choose to experience no conscious shifts as a result of your attunement, that'll be your experience.

Your unicorn guides will hold the space for you to align to the collective consciousness of their realm as well as gifting you the energetic forms of the unicorn virtues described earlier (page 35), which, as time progresses, you can grow at a deeper level. In receiving these virtues, you will become your noble Self and, in turn, become a template of nobility for others.

Your unicorn guides will also come forward to gift you your own etheric unicorn horns. One will be placed in your heart centre, one in your third eye centre and one in each of your palms. Following your attunement, anytime you focus on these, you'll automatically bring unicorn Light to whatever you're focusing on, meaning you can use your high-vibrational horns to enhance any intuitive/energetic practice for the highest wellbeing of all concerned.

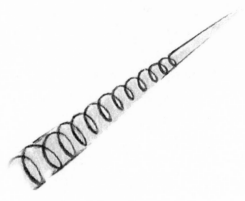

Unicorn Horn

The etheric horn as a symbol is shown above. Although it has 12 clockwise rotations, when placed within your energetic field, it spirals into Infinity to connect you directly to Source.

Everyone experiences their unicorn attunement differently. For some, the sensations are subtle, while others feel the flow of energy rise and fall within and/or around them. You may sense your unicorn guides and, depending on your path, your angelic and elemental guides, too. Often, faeries like to pop in with added sparkly goodness!

If you feel yourself getting too hot, make sure you feel connected to the Earth by visualizing roots running from your feet to the heart of Mother Earth. Likewise, if at any time you feel guided to move your body, go with this, especially if your hands want to move to parts of your body. And if you wish to lie down afterwards to help your body to acclimatize to the new energies, flow with this while giving thanks to the unicorns.

Always trust that you deserve to be linked to these wonderful beings of Creation. Just as unicorns represent divine attributes and are in service to humanity, know your own role is just as valuable. Moreover, unicorns exist beyond the constraints of time and space, so can be with many souls simultaneously. You don't need to worry about taking them away from something more important, for they are eager to work with you and assist your soul's ascension.

◊ Unicorn Attunement ◊

When you're ready to attune to the unicorn realm, read through the journey below. The attunement can take 20 minutes to an hour to receive, so it's best to give yourself plenty of time.

◊ Please choose a comfortable place where you won't be disturbed and where you can sit upright comfortably. Rest your hands on your lap with your palms facing upwards. You may feel inspired to sit in nature or to imagine yourself there.

◊ Begin with the 'Rise and Shine' meditation (page 16).

◊ Then take a few moments before listening to or reading your attunement. Breathe yourself into the moment and breathe out any questions, doubts or expectations, surrendering them to Source.

◊   Then, feeling centred, affirm aloud:

*'I am ready to receive my attunement to the unicorn realm
and affirm that this gift is perfect for me. I fully
allow the Light of unicorns to align with me.*

Thank you. And so it is.'

◊   Let go of any feelings that you should be doing
something and just enjoy this beautiful experience.

Attuning Unicorn

Feeling yourself being held in the golden Light of Source, take your attention up and through your third eye. Sense your unicorn guides standing on either side of you. As they face each other, they gently bow to touch horns, creating a luminous rainbow over you. Breathe in this Rainbow Ray, so that it fills you as much within as without. Feel yourself opening to this magical Love and receiving the healing energy of the unicorns now.

Take your awareness to your heart centre as your unicorns place an etheric horn here. This horn of light spirals out into Infinity, opening your heart as much at the front, to give, as at the back, to receive. Your heart horn links you to Creation and gifts you the virtues of the unicorns, bringing you closer to your soul. Take a few deep breaths in and out through this central channel.

Bring your attention to your third eye as your unicorns place an etheric horn here. Spiralling out into Infinity and into your deepest awareness, this horn of light gifts you the expansive vision of the unicorns, aiding you to become the ascended master that you are. Take a few deep breaths in and out through this enlightened channel.

Turn your focus to the centre of your palms as your unicorns place an etheric horn in each hand. These horns connect you to the eternal flow of Creation, supporting you to hold, channel and emit unicorn healing energy for the benefit of all. Take a few deep breaths in and out of these empowered channels as your whole being opens and expands its vibration.

Place your hands anywhere on your body where you wish to receive healing. Let the unicorn Light move effortlessly through you and allow yourself to receive whatever is best for you at this moment.

Move your hands wherever you are guided and just enjoy this loving treatment.

Know you're forever linked to the unicorns and may now channel their energy for the highest wellbeing of all concerned. Whenever you need assistance to live your truth and magic, call on them.

Relax into this bliss.

When the energy begins to wane, ground yourself on Mother Earth again by stretching your body and drinking some water.

Give thanks to your unicorn guides and their collective realm, which has now welcomed you. They are always there for you, beautiful soul. You are now as One.

#RisingReflections

- *'Attuning to unicorns is meaningful to me because...'*

- *'Their guidance concerning/healing of... is significant because...'*

- *'Becoming One with them has instilled greater faith in...'*

Soul Rising

Chapter 4
Expanding Your Senses

Everything is energy. Everything moves and is connected in its dance. You may appreciate this more after your unicorn attunement, for aligning to the Light of the unicorns helps us to recognize the underlying rhythm that weaves together the dance of life. You are a Spirit being, after all, having only a temporary physical experience. You are not apart from the rest of the world and not even 'a part' of the world – you are the power that creates worlds! And this Love-force moves through you every moment. Although on the surface life appears as matter, everything, whether it is of a material, mental, emotional or spiritual nature, is energetic. The only difference between these perceptions of consciousness is their vibratory state. For example, water always contains the same molecules of H_2O whether in its solid ice state, liquid water state or gaseous vapour state.

Like water, I believe we all have the same 'molecules' of Source within us, but when we decide to bring our consciousness into our physical body, we become an individualized expression of Creation, subject to different outer appearances but inherently the same as every other living soul. And no matter the environment we are born into or the changing conditions of our life experience, we are forever Infinite Love at our core. As we acknowledge this grace, and live from it, everything becomes accessible to us. Nothing is hidden – the secret of who we are is laid bare.

And, just as we embody Source, we naturally *give* Source to others. This is the Oneness of life the unicorns inspire us to exemplify. By doing so, we acknowledge no one is more/less than we are, including our unicorn guides. Their vibrational state is pure loving consciousness, high in its frequency but nonetheless always equal to ours, equal to who we are. And they encourage us to remember this and to see Source in all life, no matter what its outer appearance.

Love in Flow

My reiki teacher defined the word 'energy' as 'universal life-force'. Apart from this, no other definitions were provided. Instead, she explained how it moved through the chakra system and guided us to practise giving and receiving reiki to discover our own Truth. Much of what I learned was through practising and learning from my mistakes, which in my early therapist days at Ethereal Light were many!

The first reiki session I gave was for a client who had come to me after receiving reiki from another therapist. She said she had health problems but wasn't going to tell me what they were, as she wanted me to determine them. If I was successful at this, she would start coming to Ethereal Light.

Feeling overwhelmed by this, I started her session without grounding myself and throughout I remained in my ego, *trying* to see where her discordances were rather than letting them naturally arise in my awareness.

Afterwards she beamed, but I felt less than sunny. When she asked me what I had 'picked up', I shared a sense of her having irritable bowel syndrome (IBS). She looked pleased to hear this and said IBS had bothered her for years. Although my ego felt soothed by this, after she left, my stomach wrenched in agonizing knots. I'd imprinted the vibration of her IBS on myself!

If you're a healer or a natural empath (as most self-aware souls are), you may have experienced taking on the energies of other people and environments. How does this happen? In terms of efficiency, energy – or 'Love in flow' as the unicorns call it – moves through our being just like electricity moves through wires. This means it's transferable and always seeks the quickest way to ground itself, whether that's through us or through another person when we're sharing energy. And as natural conductors, when we allow our focus to be anywhere but in the present moment, we become unearthed and more susceptible to taking on frequencies instead of letting them travel easily through us.

Your Vibe Creates Your World

Science now confirms what we know in our heart to be true: everything in life is vibrational. As humanity continues to expand its collective vibe, it's becoming easier to sense this tangibly in our day-to-day lives.

Look around you for a moment. What do you see? Whether it's your walls, furniture or plants, know that everything has a living consciousness. While it's easier to feel the vibe of a plant than that of a table, the entire physical realm is a hologram – what we see as our world is a projection of our own consciousness and its state of vibration. This means that our energy affects our world and vice versa.

We can experience this truth when we share healing and when we're out in nature, for in these instances shifts in our energy are more apparent. For example, remembering the last time you were in the wilderness, did you feel yourself expanding as you experienced the fullness of your Self? At that moment (like every moment), you were projecting what you felt and were creating as the reality around you.

In the case of my reiki client, my overwhelming need to determine her ailments, coupled with the egotistical desire to alleviate her discomfort, created a reality where I received not only information about her IBS, but also the experience of it! Although she felt better, this could have been achieved without my taking on her energy if I'd remained present as a clear, grounded channel.

Because we're loving souls at our core, when we see others in pain, we want to make them better. Yet, if we're not consciously aware of our motives, we can take on their suffering just by focusing on what they're experiencing. And amid our own challenges, we can forget our divine nature and slip into feeling that life is *happening to us* rather than *happening through us*. Nevertheless, as creative souls, we always have the power to change our inner state and therefore our external projection. And there's nothing more joyful than living a physical life consciously connected to Love of who you are. For when you're aligned to this flow, you're present, fuelled by clarity of purpose, and have a zing in your step! You move through life as Life itself and even after you graduate from Earth School, you continue to exist as Life... as Love.

As I became more adept at healing, every session reinforced that as living souls, we shape our reality through our vibration. And no matter how ascended we become, or which guides we work with, there are still times when we lose touch with our Self. Then it's easier to blame something or someone for making us feel disconnected and less than we are, but this sense always starts within. Equally, the more we focus on not feeling the way we want to feel, the greater the sense of lack/fear/separation becomes. Yet, the truth is we can never separate ourselves from the divine being we are. We can only create this perception in our mind with the thoughts we're empowering and the feelings we're expressing.

When we're centred and in our joy, we know this truth. Yet when we feel tormented, such ideas are just more irritating! Over the years, I've found that during these maddening moments, it's helpful to remember that to change what we see, we must change how we feel. The best way to do this is to use a unicorn-inspired technique called 'Thank – Breathe – Reset'. Granted, this will only work when you're ready to feel better, but with regular practice, you'll find yourself reacting less and responding more, i.e. moving from feeling the world is against you to feeling empowered by knowing that you're creating your reality.

You can use this technique alone or in the company of those who are reflecting your state of vibration, otherwise known as 'the irritating-on-the-surface-yet-teacher-souls-within'! Of course, they don't need to know you're recentring yourself, edging your vibration away from lingering drama.

For a moment, hand the reins over to your ego – the inner monkey who likes to chatter and whose job it is to keep you safe and small. Allow it to grumble about something that has recently annoyed you. Don't become attached to the situation, just bring it to your awareness. And when you're ready, begin the exercise...

◊ Thank – Breathe – Reset ◊

Thank

Observe your thoughts and appreciate the monologue you're hearing. This ensures you're not trying to disguise or deny anything, or enter into any inner tug-of-wars! Simply honour this survival aspect who only wants to shelter you by saying:

> *'Thank you for sharing. I hear you, but*
> *I am willing to see the Truth.'*

Breathe

Because the mind always wants a job to do, give it the task of counting this cyclical breath:

◊ Inhale for a count of five.

◊ Suspend your breath for five.

◊ Exhale for five.

◊ Repeat three times, allowing your tummy to expand on your inhale and gently contract on your exhale.

Breathing this way centres your mind and emotions so you can connect to your soul/the underlying Truth of this situation. Long, deep breathing also produces endorphins (the feel-good hormones that soften anxiety), while cleansing your body and subconscious mind of mental conditioning and self-limiting behaviour, aka 'ego fuel'.

Reset

You've now reset your energy so it is back in the flow of Source. If you doubt this, ask your mind, 'What would it take to feel good right now?'

If you've a relentless analytic mind like mine, a 'What would it take...?' question will engage your natural problem-solving instincts while keeping you aligned to your joy.

◊ ◊ ◊ ◊

#RisingReflection

• *'I surrender the need to battle with myself and instead choose...'*

Trusting Your Intuition

According to unicorns, the greater our soul purpose to expand life, the more our ego will try to interrupt it. The ego does this because it likes the safety of what it assumes to be true. Some days my ego is like a little girl who needs reassurance and at other times it's like an auditor who delights in showing me my mistakes. While it's best to acknowledge the ego by realizing it's a product of our physiological conditioning, if we focus on the underlying Truth instead, the Light of our soul reveals itself and we become free – free to take life into uncharted waters, letting the glow of our joy light the way.

I'm not ashamed to say that I succumbed to ego chatter many times writing this book, but thankfully, my desire to share *Unicorn Rising* was greater than my fears. Hethgar came to my aid, reflecting the power of the soul to overcome the ego through loving understanding instead of denial. Your unicorn guides do this, too. For the more you lean into loving all you are, the easier it becomes to trust who you are and therefore your intuition.

The main request of students in my spiritual development groups at Ethereal Light was to understand their intuition and how best to use it to brighten their lives. Over the years, I've concluded that most people have a primary way of perceiving divine guidance, yet can develop many more ways. The Source within us does this automatically when our path changes course. For example, although my main *clair*, meaning 'clear', sense has always been claircognizance (intuitive knowing), during my scientific career, my clairsentience (intuitive feeling) became strong. And when working with KittySoaps, my clairsalience (intuitive smell) heightened.

So, whether you're an experienced energy worker or an awakening sleeping beauty, please try out the exercises that follow. They're fun and easy to do, and have been tried and tested with those spiritual development groups at Ethereal Light.

To help you get the most out of them, I'd like to share with you my 'Four Essential Steps'. You can apply these to any energetic practice, from meditation to healing to sex – if you want to have *better* sex, that is!

Four Essential Steps

These unassuming steps help to keep us present and connected with our soul, free from fear-based perceptions and receptive to the Love that is always flowing. With practice, they become seamless and automatic.

Step 1: Breathing

Breath, and its internal life-force, *prana*, literally gives our soul life within our physical body. When the last drop of *prana* leaves the body, graduation (death) occurs, resulting in the soul merging back into its greater, non-physical consciousness.

> *Take a few deep breaths now, breathing in the golden Light of Source and breathing out the same grace. Feel the Light-filled air as it flows inwards, aligning your cells to your Truth, and then flows outwards. Observe your Self in your breath, enjoying the awareness it brings.*

Step 2: Centring

Centring is placing ourselves in the middle of something else. In practice, this means bringing our focus to our heart, which many see as the 'seat of the soul'. From a unicorn perspective, the soul is not fixed within the body, yet its Love can be felt within the heart and its brilliance perceived through our third eye. Centring ourselves enables us to make the most of each moment and eases the sense of having to 'protect' ourselves when working with energy.

In my early years of giving healing, I would wrap colours around myself and call in the assistance of many non-physical beings (who weren't connected to the energy I was channelling), just to ensure that my client and I were 'safe' during our session. Then one day I thought, *If I am protecting myself, what am I protecting myself from? What is there to fear?* My inner being replied, 'You don't need to protect yourself if you come into the power of your own presence. Centre your awareness in the now and you're centred in the Light of Source.'

As I let this land within my consciousness, I realized the belief that I needed to protect myself came from my ego. It stemmed from the experience of taking on my client's health concerns and the subconscious beliefs I had picked up from others. Fear-based perceptions only arise when we look at life through a lens of duality, seeing things as light or dark and good or bad. This isn't the vantage point of Source, who is steadily neutral and guides us only in the direction of our greatest joy. Unicorns don't judge anything to be *less than* Creation either – a truth that reveals itself when we clear the mire of past conditioning and step clearly into our power.

Centred and Grounded

While there will always be protagonists and antagonists in life, when we're centred in the Love of who we are, we'll only attract the same frequency. Likewise, when we connect to the world through our heart – to live a 'now' reality – we move through life with neutrality. Self-limiting beliefs can be released, as well as anxiousness about future events.

> *To centre yourself, take your awareness to your heart. Rest there as if you're looking through your heart. Breathe in... and breathe out of your heart. If your mind wanders, don't resist the thoughts, just observe them and then take your attention back into your heart. Experience your Self, centred as the heart of Creation.*

Step 3: Grounding

Grounding ourselves on the Earth helps us to be a clear channel for energy to flow freely. In this state, unwanted frequencies can be easily released into the Earth and we can be aided in integrating the changes that best serve us.

An effective way to ground yourself is to imagine that your body, from the base of your spine downwards, is a tree. Sense your legs being a strong, stable trunk and feel roots growing down from each of your toes and the centre of the soles of your feet. Visualize those roots wrapping around the planet and connecting you to the heart of Mother Earth.

> *Take a few moments to consciously ground yourself. Give your Love to Mother Earth and feel her Love return to you. Breathe her energy up through your body, letting it fill your being, and then exhale it around yourself and feel it lifting up your space.*

Step 4: Connecting

Once we are centred and grounded, it's easier to perceive any other streams of Source consciousness we may be connecting with, like the Light of our unicorn guides. The more aware we become of what we're sensing, the more easily we'll recognize and trust divine guidance.

'I AM' statements are statements that amplify the vibrational frequency of non-physical desires, such as personal development goals or the way in which we want to live our life. Anything after 'I AM...' will create our desired destination or destiny if we affirm it with sincerity. So:

Close your eyes to connect to your soul. Affirm: 'I AM one with my soul. I AM one with Love. I AM. And so it is.'

Rest in this gorgeous state of awareness before inviting in any frequencies you want to connect with, such as your unicorn guides.

Awakening Your Senses

In our spiritual seeking, we can often look to others to define who we are and reveal our divine purpose. And while we'll always attract answers, whether they're reflected in another person or not, we can save ourselves a lot of time and money by learning to trust the voice of our soul. By doing so, we open to the loving sage that lives within us and the wisdom to enjoy radiant wellbeing. For example, by listening to our body's ailments, we can learn how to return to health. Likewise, by tapping into the emotional roots of self-limiting behaviour, we can find the means to free ourselves. With daily practice of tuning in to who we are, we'll begin to flow with that grace as the universe dutifully complies.

◊ Awakening Your Senses ◊

One of the best ways to awaken your intuitive senses is to be in nature, for nature, like unicorns, reflects the beauty of your soul. In her vastness, it's easier to appreciate your own Infinity and better intuit the living energy within all life.

So, when you're ready to enjoy this meditation, stand in a favourite spot in nature. Follow the 'Four Essential Steps' (pages 78–82), then call your unicorn guides to be with you (page 40)...

Feel your feet upon on the Earth. Breathe deeply and make the intention to unite in Love with Mother Earth. Then stretch your arms tall to the sky and breathe deeply to unite in Love with Father Sky.

On your next inhale, feel yourself breathing up Earth energy as well as bringing down cosmic energy and allow them to merge in your heart as you exhale. Repeat this sacred breath a few times and then begin to walk in nature.

Open your awareness to everything around, above and below you. Feel yourself connect to the wildlife and plantlife. Inhale the scents of the day and exhale your appreciation of being here. Open your mouth to taste the air and enjoy how the elements – the sun, wind, water, earth – greet you. Listen to the sounds around you and then tune in to the sounds in the distance. What do you hear?

Sit down in a comfy spot. Close your eyes and let the fullness of nature come into your heart. Breathe deeply. Be the awareness of this moment. Appreciate your senses and all they are expressing. Trust in them as living intelligences and know they're always guiding you to live your greatness.

When you're ready to close the meditation, give thanks to your unicorn guides and thanks for all that you have experienced.

◊   ◊   ◊   ◊

#RisingReflections

- *'Awakening my senses was a beautiful experience that...'*
- *'By using my intuition, I have more trust in myself and...'*

◊ Discovering Your Leading Intuitive Sense ◊

Each of us has a leading intuitive sense. You may already know what yours is. If you're unsure, please:

◊   Close your eyes and bring your awareness to your happiest memory.

◊   Relax and let this joyful time come forward. Witness how it takes shape.

◊   Are you instantly *there* or is it taking form around you, through images, feelings or sounds?

◊   Are you aware of any smells, tastes or textures?

◊   Open your eyes again. In what way did your memory
    reveal itself – what sense was the strongest?

Like toning a muscle, you can develop other ways to tune
in to your intuition too – it's just a matter of will and practice!

◊   ◊   ◊   ◊

Developing Your Senses

There are many ways to perceive the Love of Source, but
let's focus on those that unicorns can specifically help us to
develop. The more we practise these techniques, the more
easily we'll ascend. And as we trust the guidance of our soul
and our vibration aligns to our Source, our *clair* senses will
blend together. For example, our intuitive guidance won't
just come from our sight, but will be received through an
embodied sense of simply being our true Self. Have you ever
experienced that sense of everything in your life just flowing
in perfect timing and grace? This rapture doesn't have to be
fleeting – it can be a constant joy!

Clairvoyance

Let's look at the *clair* sense that unicorns are master teachers
of – *clairvoyance*! This way of interpreting intuitive guidance
comes through our sight, either that of our physical eyes
or our third eye. Clairvoyants can see the energy around
people and objects and their spirit guides, and translate inner
guidance through forms, patterns, pictures and symbols.

In my experience, this is the *clair* sense most of us wish to embody, but if we carry a fear of the unknown, the dark or our innate untapped potential (in truth, all the same fear), we'll struggle to develop it until we're ready to move through our shadows. In truth, there's nothing to fear in the Spirit world. It's only the 'demons' we carry that we project out into the world. If we face them, they'll dissolve. Likewise, when our divine guidance speaks to us through clairvoyance, what we perceive will relate to us, and will bring a sense of encouragement and expansion. If it doesn't, the 'Thank – Breathe – Reset' exercise (page 75) will realign our vibration with Source.

You may feel clairvoyant if...

- You see yourself as a visual person; someone who enjoys art, colour and form, and someone who notices the small details in everything, like spelling mistakes.

- You often sense images when listening to people and music or when reading books.

- You have vivid and/or precognitive dreams, which you can visualize after waking.

- You see faces and forms in things that others may bypass, like the face of a nature spirit emerging from a tree or a face formed in an abstract painting.

- You may also see sparks of light, colour or form as your spirit team approaches. These can be in your peripheral vision until you're ready to receive full impressions.

◊ Developing Your Clairvoyance ◊

This exercise should really be called 'Developing Your Uni-voyance!', for you'll be using the etheric third eye horn you were given in your attunement (page 63).

The reason the unicorns gift us a template of their third eye horn is to help us to expand our vibration to meet the wisdom of Creation. Likewise, it helps us to remember our royal Self and to sustain this dignity throughout our life. Our third eye horn also supports the recognition of our path, power and purpose, for it lets Light in, creating a high-vibrational bridge to Source. When used in any meditative, healing or energetic practices, it aids greater clarity to clairvoyance.

When you're ready, please prepare yourself with the 'Four Essential Steps' (pages 78–82) before enjoying the following...

◊   Feeling centred, bring your right index finger to touch your third eye, in the middle of your brow. Begin to trace a clockwise circle there and then continue to draw circles (at least 12) as you take your finger away from your brow. You are retracing your etheric unicorn horn and allowing it to spiral out from you into Creation.

◊   Rest your hand on your lap and, for a few moments, focus your attention on your third eye. Breathe deeply as you gently but powerfully activate your clairvoyance now. There's nothing to fear or resist – your loving soul and unicorn guides are ever-present.

◊ Staying centred, open your eyes and slowly look around your space. Don't attach to anything, just look at your surroundings.

◊ Close your eyes again. Intend that your third eye shows you what you just saw by imprinting it on your inner vision. Allow a few moments for the picture to form.

◊ With your eyes still closed, gently move your head again as if you were looking at your space. Use the power of your unicorn horn to show you everything as if your eyes were open. Don't force this to happen – take your time and trust your abilities are being refined.

◊ When you're ready to finish, give thanks to this unicorn aspect of yourself.

Repeat this exercise until your clairvoyance is as sharp as (or sharper than) your physical sight.

◊　◊　◊　◊

Clairaudience

Translating energy through your physical hearing and non-physical ear chakras is called *clairaudience*. Those with this skill easily hear the voice of their soul and can have conversations with their guides through internal dialogue. As the collective consciousness of humanity rises, it's also becoming easier for us to hear our guides through our physical ears. I'll never forget the first time I physically heard a faery – I nearly jumped out of my skin!

When clairaudience begins to develop, we may hear ringing sounds, vibrations or buzzing sensations in our head or around our ears. This is our extrasensory hearing tuning in to the frequency of Source. We may also hear words, phrases, songs, names and, in time, clear divine guidance. If at any time the sensations feel uncomfortable, we can ask for the intensity to be turned down.

Similarly, clairaudience can comfortably grow as we learn to trust and follow our divine guidance. Remember, the voice of the soul brings a sense of expansion, while the voice of the ego feels contractive. When we're centred in the present moment, if we ask our soul a question, the first voice we hear will be from our inner being and the second reply will often be the ego discrediting what we've just heard! Granted, this is frustrating, but just being aware of it can help to transcend self-doubt. With practice, you'll easily learn to distinguish what's Truth and what's distraction from the Truth.

You may feel clairaudient if...

- You're a good listener and can get to know a person just by listening to them. As well as finding communication important, you value music, pitch, tone and vibration, often hearing sounds that pass others by.

- When you read, you whisper or hear the written words. You may talk to yourself and your spirit guides often and hear melodies or songs in your consciousness as intuitive guidance.

- You prefer to listen to books and meditations rather than reading them.

◊ Developing Your Clairaudience ◊

This exercise develops your clairaudience as well as brings healing to your ears. Our ears are highly sensitive portals that can feel blocked through excessive noise pollution, negativity, gossip and abuse, self-criticism and avoiding the guidance that we know will serve us. You'll sense these areas are blocked if you have earaches or infections, feel confused when consulting your intuition or have vertigo-like symptoms. Developing your clairaudience will alleviate these symptoms and allow you to hear your divine guidance more clearly.

When I led development groups, I was often asked why the voice of our divine guidance sounded like our own voice, albeit more compassionate in tone. The answer is because we're communicating with the Source of who we essentially are. If it helps you to understand your unicorn guides better, and others in your spirit team, you can ask them to use a different tone than you'd normally use. In this way, you can better distinguish them until you trust their presence, guidance and representation of your eternal Self.

In this exercise you'll be using not only your etheric third eye horn, but also the unicorn horns that were placed in your palm chakras. These wands of Light raise your receptivity to energy while supporting you in easily holding and emitting the frequency of unicorns.

This exercise is best enjoyed in nature, where you can sit by running water or hear the wind or birds around you. When you're ready, please prepare yourself with the 'Four Essential Steps' (pages 78–82) before enjoying the following...

◊   Feeling centred, draw your third eye horn as you did in when developing your clairvoyance (*earlier*) and then trace the unicorn horns in each of your palms, too.

◊   For a moment, bring your palms together at your heart centre, feeling the unending Light of Creation moving through you.

◊   Inhale as you become this Light, then exhale it around you. Your unicorn horns, now spiralling into Infinity, are connecting you to the purest Love.

◊   Bring your palms up over your ears and keep them hovering just a little way away from them.

◊   The chakras within your ears link as one central beam that extends across your head and branches off to your pineal and pituitary glands to promote higher awareness. Focusing on this beam, allow the Light from your palm horns to gently fill this area.

◊   Next, intend that the Light detoxifies your glands and head, so that all that is ready to be recycled flows through your third eye horn straight to Source. Feel purified from the inside out as your clairaudience adjusts and ascends.

◊   When guided to do so, bring your palms together at your heart centre. Connect to the sounds of nature around you, first hearing the tones near you and then opening your hearing to more distant sounds.

◊   Meditate on these sounds as your awareness naturally expands, before closing by giving thanks and drinking some water to ground yourself.

Repeat this exercise anytime you feel bogged down by other people's 'stuff' or weighed down by self-judgement. It'll naturally clear away falseness and bring you home to your Truth.

◊   ◊   ◊   ◊

Clairsentience

Perceiving divine guidance through our feelings, often felt through our heart and solar plexus, is called *clairsentience*. Most of us are clairsentient – every moment we're interpreting energy, whether consciously or subconsciously, through our vibration. Clairsentients can also instinctively sense information through touching objects, and can feel the emotional states of people and places, too. Because many clairsentients are also empaths, they can easily pick up the vibrations of another person if they're not grounded.

Breaking Free

If you ever feel drained by someone or some place, establish energetic boundaries through deciphering where your energy stops and theirs begin. When my vibration feels heavy, I'll centre myself and ask, 'Is this heaviness coming from me or from someone else?' When my intuition says the feeling is my own, I'll use my heart unicorn horn to support myself in filtering the energy. As my heart connects to Source, I'll ask for the positive lesson of this heavy sense to come to my awareness so I can integrate what I need to know, while liberating the dense feeling.

When what I'm perceiving isn't coming directly from me, I'll ask whatever has attached to my energy field to be shown to me. Using Source Breath (page 15), I'll breathe out while visualizing golden Light moving through my entire being, evicting unhealthy attachments, and will then intend that all concerned are wholly connected to Source. This technique honours everyone and is highly effective.

If I've neglected my energy state for a while, I'll then resort to calling in Hethgar, who'll swiftly restore balance! And he's on hand to support you, too, for he is, in many ways, the Archangel Michael of the unicorn realm. Like Michael, he can also be with more than one person and in more than one place at any moment.

You may feel clairsentient if...

- You are drawn to touching textures and are naturally a tactile person.

- You find it easy to express your feelings and use your emotional experiences to support others.

- You feel the emotional and vibrational state of people, places and animals.

- You sense the underlying sentiment in art, literature, music and nature.

- You easily perceive the presence of Spirit and interpret it through emotional knowing.

◊ Developing Your Clairsentience ◊

Those who are clairsentient often carry the unicorn virtues of compassion, faith, grace and love. You can also develop these qualities by connecting to the unicorn horn of your heart. The reason the unicorns gifted this to you was to remind you of the power of Love. They appreciate that it's easy to build up barriers to giving or receiving Love through life conditions, and so gave this luminous force to you to dissolve that armour and heal all wounds so you can be the embodied Creator you came here to be. When used in meditative, healing or energetic practices, your heart horn may spiral outwards and/or inwards so that all concerned are blessed and bathed in Love.

For this exercise, you'll need an object from the natural environment, such as a stone, shell or feather. It's best you collect this yourself and don't allow anyone else to come into close contact with it.

When you're ready, please prepare yourself with the 'Four Essential Steps' (pages 78–82) before enjoying...

◊ Feeling centred, draw your palm horns to activate the unicorn frequency.

◊ Bring your right index finger to the centre of your heart centre and begin to trace at least 12 clockwise circles, moving outwards from your heart.

◊ Bring your hands together at your heart, sensing the glowing love of Creation moving through you.

◊ Inhale as you become this Light and then exhale it around you. Your unicorn horns now spiral into Infinity, connecting you to the purest Love.

◊ Cup your object in your hands and bring your hands to your heart.

◊ Focus on your object, tuning in to the feelings that come to you. Try not to engage with your thoughts, unless they're verbalizing sensations you're feeling.

◊ Continue doing this, but open your hands and eyes. Look at the object – what do you sense from it? Can you feel its vibration and physical origin? NB: If this is the first time you've consciously used your clairsentience, you may only perceive slight sensations, but this is great. Acknowledge and appreciate everything you sense. Enjoy the journey, step by step, sense by sense.

◊ When guided to do so, set aside your object and bring your palms together at your heart centre. Visualize strong tree roots growing down from you into the Earth, then close by giving thanks to all for their help and for all that was shared.

◊ ◊ ◊ ◊

Claircognizance

Claircognizance is when we receive information through an inner certainty. It's the sense of knowing something, without prior investigation, that's beyond logic. Much like a computer stores and retrieves information, intuitive data can be saved to our subconscious mind and 'uploaded' consciously at any moment. Claircognizants can receive this data in the form of blocks of thought, insights, creative ideas and action steps, all 'just known' through the crown and higher crown chakras. A few months after opening Ethereal Light, my claircognizance brought the knowing that I'd write books and even specified my publisher! At that time, I hadn't thought about being an author, yet my soul brought this certainty, which was then the catalyst of a series of events that brought me here today, sharing the Love of unicorns with you!

Claircognizants admire honesty, creativity and inspiration, and will draw on those qualities to express their divine purpose. They tend to choose a path of writing, speaking or problem-solving and to deliver their message with clear conviction.

You may feel claircognizant if...

- You tend to default to your left analytic brain, always thinking about something, having a thirst for new skills and a preference for order in your life.

- When you lose things, you quickly remember where they are. Likewise, if you feel lost, your intuition leads you to where you want to be through inspired insight and action.

- People tend to come to you for answers, especially to learn the underlying motives of people, places and situations, for you're a natural 'lie detector'!

◊ Developing Your Claircognizance ◊

A great way to develop claircognizance is to chat daily with your soul, asking questions like, 'What is the highest and best guidance for me now?' You may receive very specific guidance relating to a particular situation or general guidance like 'Keep your heart open.'

As it can take some practice to trust claircognizance, lean into clairsentience too. For example, if the knowing you receive makes your mind and heart feel peaceful, you're receiving Truth. If your heart feels heavy and/or your stomach is in knots (either excited or anxious), your ego will be distracting you from what's true. Your body will always highlight to you when you're in synch with your intuition and when you're not.

Another way to refine your claircognizance is to repeat the 'Developing Your Clairsentience' exercise (*earlier*), but before closing the space, ask the consciousness of your object to come forward. Open your heart to theirs as you ask them questions like 'What is your name?', 'What do you like about your natural habitat?' or 'What is your message for humanity?' Welcome a conversation with this being and when you feel guided to close your chat, thank them and ground yourself.

Heart-to-heart conversations with the natural world are things we'll continue to explore. But for now, let's end with the all-star exercise for developing our senses – self-healing with our unicorn guide(s)!

◊   ◊   ◊   ◊

Self-Healing with Your Unicorn Guides

Self-healing treatments with your unicorn guides is a magical and empowering experience! As you channel their Love, your soul will determine where the energy will flow. For example, healing may flow into your body, home, relationships and even finances – wherever best serves you at that moment. Because the life you see reflects your vibration, if there's an area that could be leveraged to the frequency of Source, your unicorn guides will help this to happen.

Before receiving unicorn healing, use the 'Four Essential Steps' (pages 78–82). Unicorns may appear as fluffy souls, but their power is extraordinary – think reiki on 10 cups of coffee! Being firmly rooted to Mother Earth will assist you in acclimatizing to their vibration, while still allowing anything that needs to be released and/or integrated to do so. Please read through the following guide and then enjoy this gorgeous treatment. Time just for you, beautiful soul...

◊ Self-Healing with Your Unicorn Guides ◊

◊   Feeling centred and relaxed in your heart, call on your unicorn guide(s) (by name, if they have one), by saying aloud:

> *'Loving unicorn guides, may you now channel your healing energy through me, and into me, for my highest wellbeing. May this treatment be perfect for me.*
>
> *Thank you. And so it is.'*

◊   You may feel your etheric horns activate as soon as you call in your guides. But in any event, draw your unicorn horn over your heart centre, then your third eye and then both your palms.

◊   Bring your palms together at your heart.

◊   Breathe deeply as you open to the energy of the unicorns and their Light fills your being.

◊   You can direct the flow of energy with your intention by moving your hands to the areas you wish to focus on or keep your hands together at your heart, trusting your soul will direct the flow.

◊   Gift yourself with at least 20 minutes of this uplifting Light.

◊   And when you're ready to close, bring your hands together at your heart (if they have moved) and say aloud:

'Loving unicorn guides, may you stop
channelling through me now.

Thank you. And so it is.'

◊　Give thanks for all the Love shared, before drinking some water to ground yourself.

◊　◊　◊　◊

#RisingReflections

- *'Self-healing/empowering with my unicorn guide(s) supported me with...'*
- *'Unicorn Light feels different from other vibrational frequencies in that...'*

Be at One with Creation

Chapter 5
Living Your Truth

Our intuitive senses tell us at any given moment whether we're living our Truth or edging away from it. If we always follow our intuition, we never need to turn to spirit guides for support, for we're connected to who we are. Yet, even enlightened sages dip in and out of alignment, and that's normal, in fact it's perfect, for contrast gives rise to growth. Never have we had more opportunities to grow than in our current age, for as consciousness excels itself, so too does technology, meaning it's easier now to lose sight of who we are amid the beguiling sea of social media and its draw of checking in with our phones more than checking in with our Self.

As a conscious Creator, you knew before coming to Earth that you'd explore many ways of being distracted and from that perspective, you were eager to get stuck in! From a purely physical vantage point, when you experience contrast without realizing it's the catalyst fuelling your growth, you can suffer. The key to living your Truth, therefore, is to be aware that during your sojourn on Earth you're experiencing a material life as a *human* (individualized Source consciousness) and an ethereal life as a *being* (as Source itself). In other words, using the 'life movie' metaphor, you're both the person watching the movie and the movie watching itself.

You may be among the many who are facing the dichotomy of how to live in the physical world yet be at One with Creation, too. Unicorns are responding to this in droves, showing how to bridge heaven and Earth to make every day devotional.

Journey of Ascension

Many spiritual books overcomplicate the process of ascension as we move from love forgot to Love embodied, yet unicorns are all for keeping Truth simple. While in a physical body, our consciousness explores mostly through three adventures:

1. *Soul Awakening* – living a 3D 'human'-driven life and, when our soul chooses, raising our awareness and inherent magic beyond a physical-only perspective. Here, our attention rests mainly on personal desires.

2. *Soul Discovery* – living a 4D life, where we remember our 'being' and explore different forms of spirituality, allowing our path, power and purpose to emerge. Here, our focus begins to move from *me* to *we* – to co-creative goals.

3. *Soul Embodiment* – living a 5D life, where we're refining and expanding our vibration as a unified human being,

enjoying and expressing our divine alchemy. Here, our attention rests on how best we can contribute to the Creative consciousness within all life.

Which soul state do you feel you're currently experiencing? Divine Truth is only divided by perception. Often there's a glamourized sense within spiritual communities that 5D is better than 3D, yet the viewpoint of Source is that the dimensions aren't separate, for they occupy the same space. Unicorns, too, emphasize the equal merit of all dimensions and the many possible realities between them. They can meet us wherever we are and escort us to where we wish to be, which will be to a new perception, for it's only our *perception* that defines our experience. Change your perception and you'll change your experience.

On any given day, we may feel ourselves moving through a range of different soul states, depending on the thoughts and emotions we're empowering. But when we make the conscious choice to raise (and expand) our vibration, our being – at a cellular, glandular and energetic level – starts to anchor greater quotients of Light. The greater and finer the frequency of Light we can consistently hold in our body, the more we'll naturally in-lighten, adjusting our overall frequency and awareness of experiencing a stable soul state. This is often accompanied by the realization that ascension isn't a mystical event, mode of spiritual travel or heavenly staircase we need to climb, but simply a process of anchoring into and exploring our own Infinite consciousness.

As our Light increases, our perspective widens and the sense of wanting to categorize life falls away. From an anchored 5D state, dimensions become irrelevant, for we no longer judge what's *better* or *less* than Creation; we recognize Source in all. Likewise, as we ascend, the old way of controlling life through the ego falls away.

Amid this process, it's easy to feel as though we're losing our grip on reality, for in truth, we are. We're choosing to let go of what has been to allow a new way of seeing and being to emerge. Through my own experience and service to others, I understand how daunting ascension can be, but our soul and unicorn guides are ever-present, supporting us along the pathless path and encouraging us to trust that the unfamiliar is a creative space in which we can live our magic and make our dreams our reality.

Everyday Devotion

All of us are ascending, because we all have an inbuilt drive to move ourselves forward. We can't help it – at our core we *are* Creation! Yet, through the process of descension, as we moved from Source to delineate into partial form as human beings, we forgot our sovereignty and with it became susceptible to believing we were apart from Creation. This limiting belief has kept us cycling in an incarnational hamster wheel, all the while accruing both personal and collective density that sets us apart from the Light of who we are. Now, it's time to reclaim our power as we wake from illusion, shed self-limitation and rise in harmony with All

That Is. This is the gift and process of ascension that we're now experiencing.

For a moment, visualize yourself as completely awake, aware and wholly tuned into Source – grounded in your roots and with high, open branches. See yourself unashamedly shining, radiating your Truth and Love in all directions of time, space and being. What dreams are now your reality? How different do you feel, knowing you *are* the universe? How do you think, look and act? The more you can visualize this as your reality, the more you'll manifest it. Remember, Source never judges your focus, it only provides you with more of what you're empowering through the Laws of Attraction and Creation.

The beauty of who we are is that we're all different while in physical form, thus there is no one-size-fits-all when it comes to ascension. Daily self-healing with unicorns is by far the stellar way, yet you may feel you don't have 20 minutes to spare. (Speaking from experience, when I've said, 'I don't have the time,' that really *was* the time to receive.) Nevertheless, here are some devotional ways to advance your awareness, irrespective of time or circumstance.

Sadhana Practice

While we sleep, our consciousness is wholly aligned with Source. But if when we wake we go straight into the busyness of life, we can feel the discord that results from edging away from who we are. If we don't refocus our vibration, the thoughts and feelings we are having will attract more of the same in the people we meet, the conversations we have and so on, until it's time to go back to sleep and reset our energy. The best way to allow for steady alignment throughout the day is to begin it with a *sadhana*, a Sanskrit term meaning 'spiritual daily practice'. *Sadhana* is a conscious form of spiritual fitness, which disciplines the mind and body to serve the soul. It is a space to meet, merge and grow our Godhood, not for the attainment of anything, but simply to honour the divinity within all. Through this practice, subconscious fears and limiting behaviour can be released and a greater flow brought into our life, especially if we make this gift a daily commitment.

Anything that genuinely celebrates the Divine can be your *sadhana*; for example, dancing, meditating, singing, self-healing or any other forms of self-expression that are sacred to you. It doesn't really matter what you *do*, more that you're committed. Staying devoted is saying *yes* to yourself! *Yes* to your dreams. *Yes* to rising. *Yes* to allowing your best life to emerge.

◊ Rise with Purpose ◊

The best time to enjoy a *sadhana* is before sunrise, because the angle of the sun to the Earth allows for better meditation. There's also something magical about this ambrosial time before the hustle and bustle of life awakens, when it's just you and your soul. During sleep, your nervous system has also reset itself, meaning it's primed to accept the loving vibes you'll cultivate through this practice.

Owing to the positive power of a consistent *sadhana*, negative distractions can arise, often in the shape of the derailing ego who likes to sleep more than meditate! But as you keep showing up for your Self, you'll surmount any blocks, and develop greater faith, trust and willpower.

What follows is my typical *sadhana* practice, plus other 'soul plays' inspired by the unicorns that you may enjoy. To gain the most from them, upon waking wash the back of your neck with cold water or, if you can, have a cold shower – I know, not for the faint-hearted, but a true ego-transformer and your skin and immune system will love you for it! Put on fresh clothes, preferably white and of natural material, and settle in a place you've dedicated to meditating. Keeping a sacred space set up, like an altar, to meditate at is a devotional way to honour Spirit while creating high vibes in your home. On days when I feel overwhelmed – often when I've skipped my *sadhana* – seeing my altar reminds me to pause and refocus on the most significant work of all: *alignment*. I like to place a shawl around my body too, as I feel it absorbs the vibration of *sadhana*; just putting it on helps me to get focused.

Next, I'll close my eyes, straighten my spine and bring my hands together at my heart. I'll begin Source Breath (page 15), breathing divine golden Light into my being, and then breathing it out to bridge the heart of Mother Earth and Father Sky. Resting my awareness in my heart, I'll sense my unicorn horns illuminating and then affirm aloud:

'Thank you. Thank you for this new day, a new dawn – a new way to rise and shine. I am awake – awake as I walk my path, awake as I stand in my power and awake as I express my purpose with joy. Today, I'll move through the world as Love. And I bless the world. I bless myself, my family, my home and all I take my focus to today. This is going to be a great day! For I am One with Source.'

Some mornings I'll sit in silence to absorb the Light of this affirmation before the rest of my day begins. Other times I'll add the following practices, which flow beautifully in sequence or can be enjoyed separately...

Setting a Focus

You may like to focus further on what you want to grow and move towards in your day. Or your soul may be guiding you to devote time and love to someone else. Listen to your heart and then use your creative abilities to set the tone of your day, trusting all the details will fill themselves in. For example, if you want to grow a project you're working on and receive insights to support its creation, you can envisage meaningful signs being reflected in your environment and insights flowing through your conversations, all the while trusting you'll be in the right place at the right time.

(NB: When deliberately creating in this way, if you see a rainbow or feather, or if birds seem to follow you throughout your day, thank these signs for appearing, for they're showing you that unicorns are helping your intentions come into form.)

Giving/Receiving Healing

Call in your unicorn guides to receive self-healing or send healing to another person, place or situation under the Law of Grace. This spiritual decree honours the free will ('life movie') of another being and so at soul level they decide whether they wish to receive the loving grace sent for their highest healing or not. For example, if you wanted to give the Earth healing, you could say:

> *'I send love and healing to the Earth for her*
> *highest wellbeing under the Law of Grace'*

and then visualize the world happy, healthy and wholly connected to Source.

In-Joying Life

Unicorns, like your soul, appreciate the ecstatic bliss that comes from allowing your voice and body to move freely. This way of celebrating (and enjoying) the gift of having a body naturally lifts any energetic density concerned with security, sexuality and creativity. So, whatever your favourite music is, stick it on and get grooving! By inviting your unicorn guides to join in, you may find yourself creating little ditties – take note of the words, for these are often intuitive messages.

◈ ◈ ◈ ◈

You may be thinking this is a lot to do in one morning! Don't worry, just pick what lights you up the most. By looking forward to your *sadhana* instead of seeing it as chore, you'll gain immediate gratification, and see the clarity and joy that flower as a result. Remember, *sadhana* is less about what you do each day and more about how you *live* each day. Let your spiritual practice support you in being greater than the conditions around you, so you can steadily create new patterns of health and vibrancy that benefit you. Which, ultimately, benefits all.

#RisingReflection

- *'I am going to enjoy ... as my new daily **sadhana**.'*

11 a.m. to 11:11 a.m.

Do you see the number 11 often? Or the number sequence 11:11? This is a divine sign symbolizing your alignment to Source at that moment, making 11 a.m. to 11:11 a.m. an ideal time to connect with Creation consciously.

While writing this book, I found the number 11 appearing in my awareness most days, eventually inspiring me to meditate from 11 a.m. to 11:11 a.m. with the intention of receiving a direct upload of pure loving consciousness from Source. (NB: I say 'upload' in favour of 'download', for Source lives within us and not in an external realm that we're drawing on.) Consciously asking to receive this 'upgrade' made it easier to communicate with the many celestial beings that helped to bring this book to life. As unicorns say, the greater the Light we can hold, the more we *become* that Light, expanding our awareness from individual consciousness to universal consciousness.

◊ The 11 a.m. Upload ◊

◊   If you'd like to consciously receive this progressive gift, at 11 a.m. sit where you won't be disturbed.

◊   Close your eyes and sense your heart and third eye unicorn horns illuminating and aligning with Source.

Aligning with Source

◊   With your palms open to receive, affirm aloud:

'Loving Source, may you upgrade my consciousness on all levels of being now, so I am in perfect harmony with you. Thank you. And so it is.'

This is a wholly receptive time – there's nothing for you to *do*, so simply let yourself *be* empty so you can be full of God. You may consciously feel the vibration of your bodily systems upgrading, like your immune system, or uploads of Light expanding your subtle chakras to support your ascension, or you may experience all-encompassing bliss, or feel no-thing at all. *All is perfect.*

If you can't tune in at 11 a.m., tune in when you can. What matters is your intention. Whenever you are out in nature, standing in a queue or travelling and you can safely close your eyes, open this bridge to Source. You'll prosper, and so will your environment! For example, tune in while stuck in traffic and watch how your path clears!

◊ Prosperity Mantra ◊

On days when your mind is excessively busy, give it the task of reciting this prosperity mantra from the Kundalini Yoga tradition. It'll bring about the same receptivity without mental narrative. Focus through your third eye unicorn horn as you say:

> *'Me within Me is the Purity.*
> *Me within Me is the Reality.*
> *Me within Me is the Grace.*
> *I AM the Master of this Space.'*

NB: From a unicorn perspective, prosperity has nothing to do with wealth or scarcity, but everything to do with knowing and living your Truth. To be prosperous is to stay graceful amid distractions and diversions, trusting the underlying divine order and timing in everything, i.e. accepting you'll receive what you're meant to receive in the perfect place and at the perfect time. For nothing that's for you will go by you. Embodying this wisdom will allow you to expand your prosperity on all levels.

◊　◊　◊　◊

Afternoon Tune-up

Just as we're closest to our soul before dawn, I feel we're closest to our ego around 4 p.m., making it the ideal time to get into our physicality! Often, we can feel low in mood and energy levels at this time, which fuels a foggy reach towards sweet foods (or other things we know don't serve us) to replace the 'sweetness' of soul alignment. To counter this, try this tune-up:

◊ Afternoon Tune-up ◊

◊　Come into your beautiful body to release and ground any feelings of fatigue, lack or unworthiness.

◊　Pick a workout that suits you, such as dancing, walking or yoga, to *work out* any dense foggy feelings. (I personally love weight training, for it keeps my body strong and quickly brings my energy and focus back to being in joy.)

◊ Hold the intention that this activity is returning you to your Self while it is creating the devotional space of honouring your physical self.

If you're in a situation where you can't work out but you have a moment to go somewhere quiet:

◊ Gift yourself with healing by activating your palm unicorn horns and laying them on the energy point you're drawn to.

◊ Feel yourself connect to your body through your breath, inhaling Source Breath (page 15) and using this golden Light to exhale any density and direct this energy to Source for transmutation and purification.

◊ Hold a vision of the area you're focusing on, and with it your entire being, shining with renewed Light as you come back into balance.

◊   ◊   ◊   ◊

A Little Light on Chakras

The function of our energy points – our chakras – is to draw in Source Light and circulate it around our being. As energy moves through one chakra, it flows to another through nerve channels and meridian lines, and up and down our spinal column, and through the many energetic bodies that surround and interact with our physical being.

While the chakras help us to understand our vibration, from a unicorn perspective, our system is not separated into distinct areas. For example, Love isn't just experienced through the heart chakra but also through all parts of our being. As humanity ascends, so does the way we translate energy. Slowly, we're moving away from interpreting the chakra system in terms of colour, position and quality, instead thinking of it as shifting energetic states communing with our whole being. Some ascending souls are also learning to talk to, and alter, their DNA to effect change, for essentially each cell in our body is a 'chakra', with an inner Source consciousness with which we can communicate.

Our cells, like our chakras, are intrinsically healthy; it's turning our attention away from who we are that makes us feel blocked and held in density. For example, you may perceive the energy of your sacral chakra as 'stuck' and reason this is from something that happened to you in life, or in another lifetime. While this may be valid, keeping 'in the story' keeps you out of the wellbeing that's your birthright. Instead of analyzing the feeling, ask yourself, 'What is the positive lesson and understanding behind this feeling?' This question goes straight to the heart of the dis-ease, and allows your mind-body to be heard and witnessed through the compassion of your soul. Honour and give thanks for what you receive, then ask, 'What would it take to bring myself back into balance?' Listen and take the inspired action steps that arise from this question.

Remember, your health is always just a choice away. You can empower yourself and return to vibrancy by focusing on how you want to feel or disempower yourself by staying rigid in the blame/drama of not feeling the way you want to feel. This may sound cold, but it's a warming reminder, friend, that at any moment you have the power to allow or resist the totality of your Self.

◊ Magic Nine for Sleep Divine ◊

This two-part exercise is pure gold. It positively alchemizes energy to support you in staying bright and beautiful while transforming the relationship you have with the world around you, with your significant other and with yourself. Plus, you'll have the best night's sleep ever!

Part I involves clearing the events, energies and interactions of your day, and Part II involves appreciating all the good things in order to draw more of the same to you.

Part I

It's important to wind down before sleep by detaching from everything that has filled your day. This removes the weight of the world from you and takes unwanted attachments out of your auric field, preventing you from taking dramas or concerns into your slumber.

The best way of preparing for this is to immerse your feet in cold water – yup, more cold-water therapy! Our feet are often overlooked when it comes to self-care, despite being the aspect of us that experiences the most pressure. They contain over 7,000 nerve endings, which, when stimulated with cold water, help our body to flush out the toxins and energetic attachments we have accumulated during our day. This practice is especially cleansing if you're feeling emotional and is a must for women during menstruation. Aim to immerse your feet for 15 seconds while affirming:

> *'I surrender all events, energies and interactions of my*
> *day, giving everything to Source now. [Breathe deeply*
> *to release any energetic cords.] Thank you. And so it is.'*

Part II

Feeling fresh from the inside out, get into bed to rest and enjoy the cherry on the top: *the Magic Nine*! This is a life-changing form of appreciation (when you make it your consistent practice), which wraps you in the Love of the divine. It's divided into three sections:

◊ First, list aloud three general things you have appreciated about your day.

◊ Secondly, list aloud three things you appreciate about another person. This could be your significant other, or a family member, friend or pet, or your spiritual guides. If your beloved is with you, look them in the eye as you say, 'I appreciate...' Tell them what you love and value about them, or perhaps share things you've appreciated that they have or haven't done during your day. Remember, everyone reflects You. By expressing unconditional love to another, you receive this back and everyone is blessed.

◊ Lastly, list aloud three things you appreciate about yourself. This may be the hardest of all, for often our biggest block in ascending is a lack of self-worth, which originates from the sense of feeling separate from Source. While this is illusionary, feeling alone and unworthy is very real to many. By shining Light on what you appreciate about yourself, i.e. consciously acknowledging your qualities and feeling good about all you've accomplished in your day, you will bolster your self-worth and rise in every area of your life.

◊ ◊ ◊ ◊

#RisingReflection

- *'My Magic Nine for today are...'*

Be Like a Unicorn

Another way to live our deepest and purest Truth is to be like a unicorn – to make the choice to stand radiant in our uniqueness and brave in our boldness to shatter the paradigms that say we have to be or live a certain way. We're not here to fit into another's Truth or to please Creation. Simply and magically being our Self is the greatest gift we can give the world. By being authentic, we colour the world and decorate it with the form of creativity and play that's most joyful to us.

Often, we can forget the fun that blossoms from being our true Self because we are busy 'adulting', being too preoccupied with striving for *this* or *that* to remember the innocence and wonder of our childhood and the divine sovereignty of our Godhood. But by letting our magic run free, we align with the ability to be, do and create anything that's important to us, from extraordinary relationships to unprecedented prosperity.

By allowing ourselves to be unicorn-like, we bless everything just by our presence. Our grace, kindness and talents become the Midas touch transforming limiting labels, stories and identities into our golden Self.

As Hethgar says, 'Don't limit who you are or the way you present yourself to the world. Be free – be like a unicorn! Follow what inspires you – that's how you can best serve at any given moment.'

Let Yourself Play

If we keep open to the play of life, magic ensues, and so does clearer and more expansive communication with our unicorn guides. Often, our guides inspire us to look at life each day and say, 'Let's see how much fun I can have!' And when we are in the midst of an activity, they encourage us to ask ourselves, 'How can I cultivate more enjoyment from this?' They appreciate how far humanity is out of work/play balance and want us to see the joy in our 'work' so it becomes our 'play' – to remember that it's safe (and our divine birthright) to enjoy ourselves more so we can shift our reality from 'surviving' to 'thriving'!

Unicorn Play

When I made unicorn soaps, and later wrote the Unicorn Healing® modality with Hethgar, he guided me to wear my hair down – literally to 'let my hair down' – to allow creativity to flow. For the receiving ('play' mode) of Creation is the energy of the divine feminine, and the divine masculine is the product of the creativity that arises through play. The key in balancing our life is to keep inhaling *play* and exhaling *creativity* – to give and receive unconditionally. When there's an imbalance of this exchange, we often sense lack, pain and separation in our lives. For eons, society has shone a spotlight on the masculine side of creation, the exhalation, what we can physically see and take from the world. The dance of the feminine is to be in touch with our inner child, and to connect to our magic and inner unicorn nature. It's the rise of this feminine energy that we're feeling in the world and turning to in order to heal, empower and balance our lives.

Whilst writing the Unicorn Healing® system, I also ran Ethereal Light and was actively creating the Angel Healing® and Atlantean Crystal Healing™ modalities, too. Although there was so much creativity coming through me, I often felt burnt out because the playful being of life was dominated by the work-oriented one – I was too focused on producing the physical result of what was being created. I experienced this again during the writing of *Unicorn Rising*, when I felt the intensity of the deadline rather than the peace of everything taking its natural course. So the unicorns, sensing I was in this imbalanced masculine mode, nudged me outside to receive the sun – a source of balanced masculine energy – and to play in the autumn leaves, i.e. to connect with the Earth, a source of balanced feminine energy, thereby turning my spirit back to the play of creating. They reminded me that the more we play, the more we're in our joy, and in that space everything blossoms.

For a moment, stop and think of what makes your heart sing. Do you include this joy in your daily life? Often, as awakened souls, we can give unconditionally without a thought, but when it's time to receive, we shy away and deny ourselves. If this resonates with you, ask yourself, 'What would it take for me to redress the balance in my life?' And then follow your guidance, remembering that your soul is constantly speaking to you, either directly through your conscience or subtly through your intuitive senses. If you find yourself repeatedly receiving thoughts and feelings that aren't harmful to you or another, follow them. This is your soul lighting the way.

Be the Soul of the Space

Whether you're playing, creating or washing the dishes, be the soul of that space! Meaning, put all of yourself into the moment and into what you're focusing on. All too often we feel split in our energy, pulled this way and that, building up a sense of being overwhelmed and, eventually, tired. Learn to be at peace with where you are and if ever you doubt what to turn your attention to next, ask yourself, 'What is moving me the most?' Let yourself be moved by your passion and you'll always be living from your soul, happy in the knowledge that you're exactly where you're supposed to be.

Remember, your soul is the beauty that lives within you. In this world of distractions and diversions, you may underestimate yourself and seek beauty in the external. But by working with unicorns (who are unapologetically beautiful!), you'll find it easier to carry yourself with the same grace. Then, when others come into your presence, whether you say a word or not, they'll feel your beauty and recognize it. Your Light will remind them of *home* – a home within themselves where they can unmask their beauty, too. This the power of knowing yourself, the power of knowing your soul and allowing your beauty to shine through, not to impress anyone but for the sheer joy of being true to your Self!

Kiss the Earth

We often hear about the effect of our 'carbon footprint' on the world, but what about our 'energetic footprint'? This is something that unicorns ask us to be aware of, for being human doesn't mean being independent from the world – far from it. Everything we are and everything we do creates ripples throughout the fabric of Creation.

Mother Nature

For a moment, 'feel into' your energetic footprint – what vibrations do you feel you are projecting into your home, work and social environments? Is there scope to bring greater Love to your space? In stressful/negative-feeling environments, you may want to ask Source to place 1,000 energetic gifts into your aura. Being sensitive to energy (as most aware souls are), this was something I did at the start of each working day at Ethereal Light, because some customers would come in simply to unload their problems. This technique honoured us both – my customers received Source support with what felt lacking and I maintained healthy energetic boundaries.

You may feel drawn to bring Love to the land around your home, too. Where you live is connected to your inner nature, as is the land you were born into, and thus you can bring about positive change by forming an alliance with your earthly environment. My gran was the first to teach me this through her subtle pagan-like ways, followed by the elementals and unicorns who act as ambassadors to help us to partner with Gaia so we may rise together.

Ask your unicorn guides to introduce you to the spirits of your land so you can ally with Gaia and the extensions of her consciousness known as the elements, elementals, devas, overlighting spirits and the *Sidhe*, the ancient faery souls, sometimes referred to as 'the shining ones' or 'hidden ones', within the Earth. As you greet these ancient ones, let your heart carry the question: 'How can I best help this environment to thrive?'

As we walk on Mother Earth and use her resources, we place our energy into the whole. Being aware of our energetic footprint aids the earthly beings who recycle and transform the vibrations we send out. For example, as you wash yourself, you're not just refreshing your physical body, but cleansing your mental, emotional and etheric bodies too. So, to bring support to the planet while you shower, bring unicorn Light into the water by placing your hands over the shower head and saying:

> 'Loving unicorn guides, may you bless this water as it flows over me and into Gaia now. May this healing Light bring joy to all. Thank you. And so, it is.'

Equally, when you have a bath, as the water leaves the bathtub, place your hands over the plughole to bless the water as it returns to the Earth.

As you move about your day, kissing the Earth in these ways and any others that are meaningful to you, offer Love to yourself, too. By embracing who you are, you walk as Source in body, blessing all and uplifting all through your unique perspective and divine blueprint.

Envisaging your heart being open at the back to receive from Creation and open at the front to give to the world creates unending bliss and is also a wonderful habit to develop. Your magic, love and kindness can then flow unconditionally to those you encounter, especially to your greatest teachers, i.e. those who poke and provoke you beyond your limits in order to reflect that you're limitless.

Soul Food *vs* Ego Fuel

Keeping our mind and body as pure as we can without denying ourselves results in expansive vibration and radiant wellbeing. This is an individual process. While we're in physical form, we're all unique in our biochemistry, meaning the best diet for us is one that come to us through our intuition.

If you feel you could improve your diet, ask yourself, 'What foods fuel my soul/my wellbeing?', 'What foods fuel my ego?' and 'What would it take for me to improve my lifestyle?' Write down the answers.

Like so many of us, I've had a challenging journey with food. After navigating my way through bulimia, I became an emotional eater, reaching for foods that gave me physical comfort as a substitute for the soul alignment my being was really reaching for. It wasn't until I asked those questions that I realized how imbalanced my diet was. Not in terms of food groups, but in what I was energetically supporting. For it's not *what* we eat that essentially causes us dis-ease or weight gain, it's *how we feel* when we eat the foods we do. For example, I used to hide the fact that I was eating milk chocolate because I knew my system was sensitive to dairy and I didn't want to face the scorn, however playful, of my partner. The sweetness of the chocolate was fleeting, yet the guilt and shame I was also consuming were long-lasting.

So, the key is being aware of your energy state as you eat (and prepare) your food, while also finding a soul-food/ego-fuel balance, so you're not limiting yourself. A little ego fuel is okay, for it keeps mental chatter at bay, even more so if what you're eating conjures up joy. For example, I'll often cook apple crumble because my gran made it for me when

I was young. Enjoying this dessert always makes me think of the happy times we spent together and so, even though apple crumble isn't very supportive of my wellbeing from a nutritional perspective, it's more 'soul food' than 'ego fuel' to me!

The Unicorn Diet

From a unicorn perspective, the most optimal foods to bring into your diet are what they term 'original foods', i.e. those with little or no influence from other energies before consumption; for example, foods you've grown, picked and cooked yourself. These will benefit your system best, especially if you have a personal affinity with their supporting land.

A step beyond this is what unicorns term 'primary foods', i.e. those that you haven't produced personally yet still originate from the earth, such as fruits, vegetables, grains and nuts.

Other foods, like meat and dairy, are still beneficial, but they're another step away, being 'secondary foods'. Furthest yet is processed food.

This fresh take on holistic eating makes sense if we look at the pattern of development that many people follow as their consciousness ascends. First they cut out processed foods, then meat, then dairy, then navigate towards a raw diet and lastly, they may even adopt a water-only/breatharian existence. Although a water-only diet may sound extreme (and should only be undertaken with the appropriate supervision), there are some souls for whom this is now an everyday reality. As every generation ascends, the collective consciousness of humanity and of planet Earth are slowly supporting the next generation to enjoy a more 'original' diet, creating the opportunity to grow our own food and, if it's for our highest wellbeing, to advance safely into enjoying a breatharian lifestyle.

That said, Source never judges our diet. When someone chooses to eat meat they're not 'lower' in spiritual merit than someone who eats only fruit and vegetables. And so you may wish to balance the unicorn guidance with listening intuitively to what best serves your body. For example, sometimes I'll crave meat during menstruation. Whether my body wants the vitamin B12 (an essential nutrient mostly found in meat) or just wants the 'grounding' to match the density of what I'm releasing is irrelevant. What's important is that I trust the intelligence of my body. In the past, I've not eaten meat when my body has prompted it for fear of external condemnation. Yet, everything has consciousness and so we can't deem the eating of meat to be wrong when we're growing vegetables then taking them away from their home and consuming them, too.

What we can all do is honour our food by appreciating its consciousness, and thanking it and the earth, elements, elementals, farmers and other souls who have aided its development. To do this, consciously breathe (using Source Breath) on your food to give thanks to it and to expand its frequency. This is especially beneficial when the only food you have is something you feel isn't the best for you or if you're eating food someone else has prepared. Their vibration isn't 'bad'; it's more that you're suffusing the food with your own specific energetic signature so it best supports your system.

You can also raise the vibration of food whilst preparing it. Through attuning to unicorns, you may find yourself singing and dancing when cooking – this is a loving way to gift others with true *soul food*, too!

#RisingReflection

- *'I allow myself the freedom to be like a unicorn – to be more playful, present and aware of my energy in the environment! I see this improving my health and lifestyle in the following ways...'*

Unicorn Heart

Chapter 6
Pain is Temporary, Love is Constant

The relationships we experience in life, beginning with the family we choose and moving to the friends we have and the bond with a significant other, may feel like a varied mix of 'the good, the bad and the ugly'. Yet our relationships enable us to grow and, as we become more aware, reflect on whether we're allowing the totality of our unicorn Self to emerge or stay the same amid a cosy crowd of horses. Through the eyes of Source, there's no judgement of the choices we make/don't make, but we know our soul is here to expand and expand it will. And as we rise, we can't expect our relationships to stay the same.

Attracting Our Unicorn Tribe

Another side effect of growing in spiritual awareness is recognizing our Self in others. On the surface this may appear to be egotistical, but it's a way of embodying connectedness with our fellow Earth brothers and sisters – a way of honouring the Light within them and acknowledging that the same radiance lives within us.

As we expand our perception, it's easier to see the Light in all and, through this recognition, to attract the presence of kindred soul mates and soul family members. These are individuals with a similar purpose and outlook to us, with whom we've incarnated before. As the saying goes, 'your vibe attracts your tribe', meaning being authentic draws in those who see us and who want to support us in living our best life.

We'll know when we meet someone in our soul group, for we'll share an inextricable connection. We may have a soul contract with them, too. A soul contract is an agreement we make before incarnating. In theory, every interaction we have in our life stems from a soul contract, because every encounter we have with someone is either to fulfil the purpose of supporting them, or to have them support us, or to foster a joint goal. Whether soul contracts deal with relationships, events or choices, their aim is always for us to grow.

As unicorns can bridge dimensions, we can ask them to show us our soul contracts and with whom they're linked. If we do this in meditation, they'll invariably guide us to our Akashic records to read our soul agreements. Whatever covenants you've entered into, friend, embrace them. Trust in the wider view of your Self as you open to the magic that ensues from letting pacts play out.

When I hired my first manager for Ethereal Light, we instantly connected and felt another life connection. As we started to work together, we realized we had a soul contract to support the growth of the centre. Often we'd tune in to our contract, both of us seeing our souls like mischievous faeries eager to play out the pact we'd created. But although my manager was a gifted psychic, I later learned she was also dishonest. I didn't want to acknowledge the extent of it, for we'd become close friends. But as she left the centre, I realized this was part of our contract, too. Though I was feeling wounded, she had helped me to stand in my power – confidence I'd signed up to receive. Along with the strength needed to embrace the Light of my new manager, who happened to be my twin flame – the romantic counterpart to my soul.

Twin-Flame Union

A couple of years prior to meeting my physical counterpart, I was sitting with two spiritual friends talking about our relationships. One of my friends said her fiancé was her 'twin flame' and ranked twin-flame union as superior to soul-mate relationships, believing a person could only have one twin and it was rare to find them in the same lifetime.

As this was the first time I'd heard of this concept, I was eager to learn more and asked her, and our other clairvoyant friend, to tune in to my twin to bring his consciousness forward. He graciously agreed to our request and as he emerged, we could all sense his energy. His vibe felt like fire, but as it settled there was a calm undercurrent of the ocean, too. It felt like *home*.

I asked my friends, 'Do you feel my twin flame is my current boyfriend?'

They looked at each other, trying not to disappoint me as they telepathically confirmed the contrary.

'Oh well, it was a long shot,' I said, feeling slightly let down.

Before going to sleep that night, I called in my twin flame's consciousness and immediately felt him envelop me. The vibration was slightly stronger this time, but it had the same elemental feel as earlier. It was beyond anything I'd experienced before. In the weeks and months that followed, I invoked this beautiful soul to cuddle me to sleep.

At this point in my life, Archangel Michael and his divine counterpart, Archeia Mikaela, featured strongly. We were busy crafting angel workshops and the Angel Healing® programme together. Michael laughed at how ridiculous it was lying physically in bed with my boyfriend and energetically calling in someone else! Yet, I was captivated. And the more I leaned into my twin flame, the more I wanted him to be present physically.

'You have to make room in your life for him to enter,' Mikaela said, knowing this meant working less and allowing more, as well as ending my current relationship.

As I took this leap of faith, my angel and unicorn guides helped me to get ready to receive him, because twin-soul union manifests in the physical world when both partners have reached a point of loving themselves enough to attract each other vibrationally.

Manifesting into Physical Reality

To manifest something into physical reality we must realize that 'reality' is the spiralling dance of two worlds: *manifested reality*, the reality we walk upon, and *vibrational reality*, the reality that is always in a state of becoming. In other words, what we see around us now is the physical result of what we've allowed for in our life and crafted through our conscious and subconscious desires. Yet, it isn't the totality of our life. From the vantage point of our soul and guides, our material world is yesterday's news, for our non-physical Self is focusing more on the vibrational reality we're creating. The more we understand this, the more we naturally synch with our vibrational reality, making it easier to be deliberate about manifesting what's important to us.

With regard to my twin, I could clearly sense his vibrational reality. Yet, this felt frustrating when I focused more on the lack of his physical presence than on trusting that he would appear in my life at the perfect time for me to receive him. To help me, the angels and unicorns said to stop wishing and hoping he'd appear, and instead feel the joyful expectation that he *was* coming into my life – in fact, vibrationally, he was already *there*!

Manifesting

As personal wants were surrendered, my frustration melted like a cooling breath mint, helping me to breathe deeply into the knowing there was nothing for me to do other than believe that if this path was highest for me, it would blossom.

Returning to trust inspired a daily *sadhana* of self-love, which in turn dissolved the sense of needing another person to fulfil me. And the irony was, the more I let go, the more I felt my twin's presence! Through loving myself more, I learned to detach to the outcome of his appearance and instead just enjoy the fun of imagining him in my life. For example, whilst watching a movie, I'd often see him with me, both of us snuggled up eating popcorn and laughing at silly jokes.

Imagining doing mundane activities with him helped to ground the spiritualized illusion that my soul was missing a piece. Likewise, keeping present helped to assure my heart and mind (the bridges between our vibrational and physical reality) that everything was in perfect flow.

◊ Treat Every Day as Your Birthday ◊

By expecting your intentions to materialize physically, you're teaching your being that trust is your default setting. The more you allow your consciousness to synch with Source, the more quickly your manifestations will appear and the more allowing your vibration will become. Every time you receive what you expect, it's a wink from Creation to remind you of what becomes possible when you trust and surrender.

Try this for yourself now:

◊   Think about something you want to appear in your life – a small goal you aren't attached to. For example, ask for a surprise gift to come into your day.

◊   Now close your eyes and rest in your heart, visualizing your third eye and heart horn spiral to Source.

◊   Remember a time when you knew something amazing was about to happen. Feel, with all your being, that anticipatory sense, like magical butterflies dancing within you.

◊   Physically open your arms out wide and be like a child who sees the world as vast, loving, kind and Infinite.

Let the universe shower you with presents as if it were your birthday.

◊　Manifesting like this keeps you light and buoyant with the expectation that your surprise (or whatever you asked for) will appear by the end of your day.

NB: Creation never judges what you're asking for; it's only your focus of attention that determines what you receive. If you're more focused on already having what you're creating, rather than its perceived lack, your intentions will come to fruition. Similarly, your degree of trust is proportional to the speed with which your manifestations move from your vibrational to your physical reality. As you embody this, you'll see the material evidence accrue and with it, anchor greater faith that you're the Creator of your reality. The key, whether manifesting small gifts or large dreams, is to play this creative game in the same way – having faith that everything is evolving for your highest wellbeing and having no attachment to how or when things appear.

◊　◊　◊　◊

#RisingReflection

- *'I allow myself to be light, playful and receptive in this manifesting game, knowing that as I participate, I perfect!'*

Recognize the Driftwood

It took me two years of manifesting my twin to understand how to bring things into form and so, friend, I empathize if you're frustrated your big dreams aren't physically in play right now. Keep the faith and watch for signs, for signs are the driftwood that show that your ship *is* coming in.

My driftwood appeared in the form of many men! Archangel Michael assured me my twin would appear in one of my workshops. Because the only men who generally came to my classes were gay men or gentlemen over 60, I doubted him. Yet doubt didn't stop me from neurotically thinking that every man who came into Ethereal Light was my other half!

Around this time, I shared the first Unicorn Healing® practitioner course. It was such a loving day, attracting the most beautiful souls. The content was written into teaching manuals but, ever true to the unicorns, we alighted from those and went with what was flowing. I found myself leading everyone into a circle, where each person in turn sat in the middle to receive unicorn Light from everyone else in the group, as well as healing and messages from their soul and unicorn guides. When I sat in the circle for healing, an etheric being came into view in the guise of a five-year-old girl with long blonde curly hair and defiant yet loving energy. She called herself Rowan, and said she was the child I was destined to have and that she was preparing for her sojourn on Earth.

To say I was taken aback would be an understatement! I hadn't thought about having children, especially coming from a single-parent family and witnessing the challenges I had. But this soul was so expectant about coming in. After the healing, half of the group shared that they had sensed her and the clear message that she was destined to be my child.

From then on, Rowan appeared often, coming into my awareness with information about our lifetimes together and insights for my classes. Together, we created profound inner-child meditations and loving ways to inspire others to enjoy the play of life, much as unicorns do. For Rowan's soul was elementally connected to the unicorns in inner Earth and to the off-world species, and as such had great wisdom to impart.

At work one day, I read the attendee list for an upcoming Archangel Michael workshop and as I read, 'Jonathan' I simultaneously heard Michael say, 'He is your counterpart,' and sensed the excitement of Rowan confirming this, too.

On the day of the workshop, I was in the centre's shop greeting participants as they arrived. As Jonathan approached me, I felt his familiar vibe. Although I'd romanticized the idea of twin flames, the moment we met did feel like a fairytale. As our eyes met, everything else faded from view – we created a bubble within our own dimension.

Trying my best to set distraction aside, I started the workshop and during the last meditation, Rowan came in and sat defiantly on Jonathan's lap, remarking to me, 'Look, it's Daddy!' I tried not to giggle, for her energy was so spritely!

At the end of the meditation, Jonathan shared his feedback. Right at the end, he added, 'Oh, and the strangest thing happened – I felt a little girl pulling at my trouser leg and then sitting on my lap.'

At this point I did laugh and after we began dating, I told him this story and how his higher Self had been around me for two years. What made this even more intriguing was he said he'd met my spirit before our physical meeting, too.

The Greatest Love Story of All

Let's look at the concept of twin flames from a unicorn perspective, for they remind us that the greatest love story of all is the Love story of our life and our most significant other is our divine Self.

For eons, we've been conditioned to believe that in order to feel loved, we must 'find love' in the form of another person. If that person tells us they love us, then we've been successful in gaining love, and if they say they don't love us, we have lost love. Yet, Love isn't something we *gain* or *lose*, it's who we *are*. Living life is living Love, and so we must be gentle and tender with life as if carrying it like a babe in arms, adoring it for the miracle it is. Somewhere along the spiral, we've forgotten this and now, in many spiritual communities, the highest form of love is regarded as twin-flame union with another person. This idea suggests that our soul is split in two before it enters the incarnational cycle, with one half seeded in us and the other half in another person, and if we've raised our consciousness enough to meet our 'other half' physically, then our union makes us whole.

While this may be true for some, what I've gleaned through my experience of meeting, manifesting, merging with and then physically separating from my twin is that this is a very spiritualized codependent view, which can limit a person from embodying wholeness from the inside out.

Unicorns never limit or label Love, only experience it and celebrate its bliss. They remind us that all paths lead to God and so all paths lead to embodying the Love of God. They see 'twin-flame union' as the marriage of the divine masculine and divine feminine Light within us, aka the merging of our human self and creative Self.

This means we can experience embodied Love without another person. Yet, if we wish to experience this joy with another person, we can by asserting that our significant other is our 'twin' – we don't have to wait for *the* one. Any romantic partner we share a love connection with (aka a strong vibrational harmony with) can be our soul's counterpart. So, if you're in a relationship and your beloved is willing to be your soul's counterpart, simply affirm it is so with your creative will. And then enjoy, through this sacred contract, the experience of soul union as you give/receive the divine masculine, feminine or unified blend of Source Light to best facilitate the healing and learning necessary to embody wholeness from the outside in.

This fresh perspective explains why our unicorn (and angelic) guides project their vibration in either a feminine or masculine form to support us in balancing and uniting with our Godhood. The merging of the feminine and masculine aspects of Creation has nothing to do with our physical sex organs or the gender we identify with, but is a state of universal alignment with Source – a state of self-actualization that results from integrating our heart and mind into the Love of who we are.

The desire to enjoy romantic love with another person is part of the gift of human life, but it's crucial (for our happiness and sanity!) not to be dependent on another person to fulfil us. Rather, we should see them as the 'cherry on top' of an already epic Love story. And then, to gain wholeness with them, focus on what we can co-create that serves the world.

If you think like this, it will help you to open to Creation in a whole new way and enjoy the bliss that'll unfold. And so, whether you see your soul as having a divine other half, or are affirming that your romantic partner is your counterpart, or are simply viewing this as a metaphor for moving from single-minded living to helping to create a better world through personal unification is of no consequence, for Love will emerge in the heart of all of your relationships.

This can be expedited if you appreciate that everyone is a conscious expression of God, a living sacredness within the world. And when you come together with them, whether in a romantic pairing or a brief encounter with a stranger on the street, value the sacred in your alliance.

◊ The Marriage of Divine Love ◊

Twin Flame Union

The unicorns would like to share a sacred practice that brings about unity on all levels. It can be adapted and enjoyed in three different ways:

◊   By marrying your human self to your higher Self.

◊   By strengthening your relationship with your physical beloved.

◊ By creating the space to attract your most compatible partner/twin flame/soul mate, and meet and merge with their higher Self to accelerate their physical manifestation.

The first way supports you in internally balancing your divine masculine and feminine energy, dissolving any barriers to fully loving who you are. The second and third ways help you to do this too, but also gift the experience of Love in the form of meeting and merging with your physical beloved. Have fun exploring the way(s) that speak(s) to you and, if possible, enjoy this just before sleep.

Following your Magic Nine practice (page 118), or in a state of relaxed awareness, sit with a straight spine and rest your hands, palms up, on your lap.

Call in your unicorn guides (and the unicorn guides of the other person, if applicable) to kindly hold a clear space that honours the highest intentions of everyone concerned.

Sense your unicorn heart horn spiralling outwards, emitting a beautiful iridescent Light.

Imagine your beloved is in front of you and sense their unicorn heart horn radiating the same Light.

As you open your hearts to each other, imagine the Light from your horns touching, activating Love on all levels.

Breathe into this sacred heart of Creation as you merge with your significant other, becoming as One now.

Stay in this bliss for as long as you wish, then gently intend that your unicorn horn spirals back into your heart centre.

Thank the unicorns and the grace of your partner.

If you wish, set your intention to meet your other half while you sleep to deepen your relationship even more.

If you're using this technique to manifest your most compatible love, there may be a tendency to list specific attributes that you'd like to see in them. While knowing what you want is wonderful, too many specifics can slow down their arrival. They'll show up sooner if you focus instead on how you'd like to feel in their company. For example, if you expect them to be funny, say to yourself as you open to them, 'In your company, my most compatible and attuned love, I'll feel uplifted through our laughter and play.'

Always create from the inside out with the intention that your physical union will serve the world.

◊　◊　◊　◊

From Self-Abuse to Self-Love

One of the greatest lessons I've learned so far is that when I love myself, I love the world and it loves me right back. I unapologetically accept from life and feel deserving of its many blessings.

Arriving at self-acceptance has been a long journey and some days I'll navigate away from my Self. Yet, those are revealing times, when my soul shows me where I'm limiting the flow of Love.

When we break the barriers we've built against Love, we are free. But for years I hid behind those barriers. Through experiences of sexual abuse, I was ashamed of myself and self-harmed to distract myself from my pain. I became a master of self-sabotage, enjoying the relief that came from comfort eating, bulimia, and drug and alcohol use. These 'temporary fixes' helped to mask the trauma of my past, but as I became more aware, my guides reminded me, 'Through your greatest challenges, you find your greatest strength. Remember, you can choose to feel a victim of your past or rise now in your power.'

Then I saw the extent of my victimhood and how I'd let myself live in the density of my story, keeping my heart closed for fear that opening it would lead to further abuse. Because our ego only replays our history, it fears the repetition of events, saying anything to keep us (really, *itself*) safe. Embracing this Truth allowed compassion to flood in, softening fears in its wake and enabling Love to re-emerge.

◊ Embodying Love ◊

◊   Listening to your heart, do you feel you're embodying Love in your life or turning away from it?

◊   Is it easy for you to accept Love and share it unconditionally with others?

◊   If not, what would it take you to restore balance?

As you ask yourself these questions, honour the Truth your heart shares, for your heart will never lie.

Another restorative question (especially for challenging life moments) is to ask yourself:

◊   'How can I bring more Love to this situation?'

Because Love detangles all, either giving, receiving or being a lighthouse of Love can lay to rest any resistance that shows up in your life. For instance, if there's something troubling you right now that you feel you can't resolve (or let go of) ask:

◊   'Do I need to give, receive or be Love in this situation?'

Your heart will share one or more ways to help to harmonize the situation. If it doesn't, follow the 'Rise and Shine' meditation (page 16) then ask this question again, consciously listening and applying the advice you receive.

#RisingReflections

- '*In the following relationships, do I need to give love, receive love or be Love to enjoy greater harmony and wellbeing: with myself, with my significant other, with my family, my friends, my home and my relationship to Source?*'

- '*What actions (if any) do I need to take to enable loving shifts in these areas?*'

Finding Love after Loss

Just as unicorns help us to align to Love in our relationships, as well as embody Love in all facets of our life, they can also help us to heal after feeling the loss of love. They remind us that the greatest growth our soul can experience through being human comes from how we relate to our consciousness at these moments.

As our soul descends from Creation through the veil of amnesia into the denser levels of material matter, we first learn to love ourselves, then to love our significant others and then to love Source, which weaves together the tapestry of all life. Like embroidery, if we just focus on loving ourselves, we light up just one part, but as we extend our heart to others, to the world and to Creation, we light up the whole design and everyone becomes blessed. For living life is living (and sharing) Love.

When you feel worn down by loss, despite knowing you can never *lose* love, you owe it to life to get back up, to open your heart again and to rise like the beautiful phoenix you are.

After a wonderful few years, my relationship with Jonathan came to a physical end owing to the blanket of codependency we'd skilfully woven together. Although the break-up took me to my lowest, it also helped me to lean in more to Spirit, to nature and to my friends, which all too often we don't do for fear of being vulnerable. Yet, it's through sharing our vulnerabilities that we re-emerge, healed from the lesson of heartbreak, wise in our willingness to strip away self-limitation and stronger in our capacity to love anew.

Sitting in the bath one evening a few months after our break-up, I still felt broken-hearted as I mourned the loss of not just my best friend, lover and teacher, but also a portal of divinity that I'd placed high on a pedestal. I called in spiritual support to help me to go to the root of my pain and to envelop in Love what needed to be heard and healed.

In answer to the call, I was drawn to give healing to myself from the moment of conception to my birth. Before I knew it, the scene changed to healing my mum as she carried me through the pregnancy. I felt the violent attacks of my father on us both and then saw many angels gathering around my mum when she was giving birth to me. And many midwives, too – there were six of them. My dad wasn't present, just this force of feminine energy. I could feel my mum's heartbreak and as the tears streamed down my own face, my heart and her heart became One. Both of us, plus my dad, were receiving Peace at that moment. I hadn't known anything in detail about my conception or birth, or how my mum had felt after I was born, but then it all became clear.

The next day I shared this vision with my mum and she confirmed what I'd seen, even the six midwives! This experience was so deeply reconciling for us both that I wondered what positive shifts could manifest through healing the whole of my timeline. Could other traumas be laid to rest, as well as fears and phobias? And what if I invited others to join me in this healing adventure – what could we create together?

This was the moment the *12 Days of Love* was born – a free global healing event where I and 1,500 others gathered online from 1 December to 12 December 2012 to heal our timelines from our earthly conception to our current age. Owing to the great shifts in consciousness we experienced, I received countless emails from participants sharing how they'd healed deep-seated traumas, fears and doubts, and gained the peace, love and clarity to move forward in their lives.

This event was equally as transformative for me. It enabled me to visit my dad and forgive him for his behaviour and his absence from my life. This in turn helped me to forgive Jonathan and heal the perceived loss of the divine masculine that I felt he, among others, had removed. At a macro level, it allowed for a more meaningful, trusting relationship with Creation. And on the day of reconciliation, I also found the courage to tell my mum about being raped, which then dissolved the shame of the divine feminine I'd also been carrying.

A space of freedom was created within me. It was safe to be seen, safe to let the past go and safe to shed the suffering that had been preventing Love from flowing freely in my life. I realized how much I'd been fighting myself and those who represented my pain. I didn't need to fight now – I was free at last.

The Meaning of Healing

What does 'healing' mean to you? Through the eyes of unicorns, it is seen as a return to our Self through accepting who we are and letting go of what we're not. It's a process of shedding the experiences and stories we wear as our identities in order to enjoy the gift of life fully.

Having healed from the universal challenges of pain, loss and trauma, I appreciate the courage it takes to love yourself enough to be seen and, more so, to express your Self without censure. But when we realize that our healing needs our co-operation, we can then allow more of what serves us and therefore the world as well. We can never change past events, but we can change the way we feel about them. Equally, we can never address the accountability of those who've hurt us, but we can release ourselves from victimhood by using our compassion. This, coupled with forgiveness, can free us from denser energies held within our body, replayed by our mind and felt as our emotions. This gentle shift profoundly helps us to change the vibration of how we see past events, thereby positively affecting our current energy state.

If you've experienced trauma connected with an abuser, recognize that when you make it your dominant intent to empower yourself, that person cannot hurt you any more. Try to look at them with compassion. When I learned of my dad's violence towards my mum, I couldn't manage the hurt this created. I was too young to understand why someone who was 'my dad' would hurt another person, especially his beloved. As I distanced myself from him, I attracted men like him into my life. However, this pattern stopped when I intentionally chose to empower myself through the *12 Days of Love*. By bringing compassion in, I could face my inner hurt and extend Love to my dad. I imagined walking in his shoes and looking at what had happened in his life to compel him to be abusive, while knowing that at his core, he was, and is, Love.

As no one is born malicious, it must be the conditions we face in life that influence our behaviour. My dad's conduct was something he'd learned and then facilitated even more through years of drug use. By embodying compassion, I saw the Divine within him and witnessed, through the eyes of Source, the life movie he'd chosen for himself. As I made peace with this, my energy lightened and the ancestral line of abuse ended.

Through the *12 Days of Love* meditations, I've also realized there's no such thing as karma in terms of affecting what appears in our reality. From Source perspective, our soul is pure, loving consciousness and when we enter physical life, we do so without any baggage. We may enter (with purpose) a genetic and ancestral line or a particular environment to effect change and carry soul contracts agreed before our incarnation, but we don't have any 'debts' to pay from other lifetimes. This is another outdated, limiting concept that our collective Light is ready to liberate. For all the things that have happened will happen and are happening to do so in the present moment. Sometimes we can fool ourselves into thinking a particular circumstance is manifesting owing to another life scenario. Yet, the unicorns steer us away from such imaginary entrapments by reminding us to trust what feels True and to leave the rest.

This image below shows an open doorway that represents the portal we journey through as we heal our timeline in the *12 Days of Love.* All levels of healing (no matter dimension, timeline or level of perception) are forever accessible to us but we must be prepared to walk through the door to our own healing process.

◊ 12 Days of Love ◊

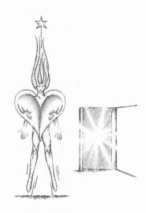

Self-Love

The masks of our past often hinder us from being fully present and available to Love, whether we're consciously aware of these identities (and their fear-based limitations) or not. This heart-opening technique is a way of transforming such masks from the moment of your conception to your current age, so you can be wholly your Self and not your experiences.

> Over 12 meditation sessions, your inner being and spirit team will hold a space of healing and empowerment for your younger self. Even though time is not linear, when you give Love to your younger self, you immediately change your current reality through a process of divine alchemy. Through holding this safe, unattached space, it becomes easier to accept, forgive, let go of and/or integrate the energies that are influencing you to be less than your shining Self, leading to a profound transformation in all areas of your life.
>
> Before beginning the *12 Days of Love*, please divide your lifetime into 12 daily meditations, from your conception to your current age. For example, if you're 44 years old, you could split your sessions as follows:
>
> ◊   Day 1: Focusing on the time from conception to birth
>
> ◊   Day 2: From birth to the age of one
>
> ◊   Day 3: From one to four
>
> ◊   Day 4: From four to eight
>
> ◊   Day 5: From eight to 12
>
> ◊   Day 6: From 12 to 16

◊   Day 7: From 16 to 20

◊   Day 8: From 20 to 24

◊   Day 9: From 24 to 30

◊   Day 10: From 30 to 34

◊   Day 11: From 34 to 40

◊   Day 12: From 40 to now

Once you've created your plan, set aside 12 days in your diary so you can commit to enjoying the meditations consecutively. Give yourself at least 30 minutes for each session.

◊   When you're ready, begin a self-healing session with your unicorn guides (page 100), but this time, ask the unicorns to support you in bringing healing to the part of your lifetime that you're focusing on. For example, for Day 1, sense your younger self, from conception to birth, being bathed in divine Love.

◊   As beliefs, emotions and memories arise, don't become attached to them, just witness what's happening and breathe, allowing what needs to transform consciously to do so in its own time. Remind your younger self how loved and supported they are, and as you get ready to end the meditation, sense this portion of your life being wrapped in the golden Light of Source.

◊   Let go of anything that is less than Love and then close the space with reverence, giving thanks to all

who have supported your meditation and drinking
some water to ground yourself.

◊   Note your experience and then repeat this process for
the other days, adjusting your focus each time to give
healing (and hold sacred space) for every portion of
your life's timeline.

(If you'd like to enjoy the original *12 Days of Love* video
series, you can find it, plus an in-depth introductory clip,
on my YouTube channel at http://bit.ly/2gIAHFe.)

◊   ◊   ◊   ◊

Mary Magdalene

Chapter 7
Embracing Your Quest

When we stop learning, we stop living Love. By keeping curious, we keep aligned to our soul and transparently grow through what we go through. The learning and understanding of each life moment can transform victimhood, self-limitation and fear in their crystal-clear wake, making it easier to trust our path through grounded, present roots and easier to express our purpose through a vibrant vibration. Then the great Truth can be revealed – that our quest in Earth School isn't to know heaven, it's to experience heaven *through* Earth, through our physical body, so we can walk boldly as a divine human being while learning how to walk joyously with others. For we're all here to be *human*, but we're also here to be a *being*, too, and there's equal divinity to both aspects of Source. So our life quest teaches us that it's safe and natural to be seen, heard and loved and to give Love as we expand life beyond what's been before.

Becoming Empowered

The path to personal empowerment equates to the path of personifying our divinity and, like the Love that creates worlds, is irreversible. Once empowerment is anchored, trying to return to an old perspective is like riding a bicycle backwards – technically possible, but not especially enjoyable!

Unicorns are graceful masters at holding their Light high, and they reflect our capacity to enjoy the same confidence by letting go of the perceptions and stories that have been leading our life and taking our power back. This means saying farewell to 'This is the way it's always been', and 'This is how my mother/father/teacher taught me to be', and 'I don't have the means to change my life', and letting our Self steer.

Gaining the courage to walk this road less travelled will lead us to understand ourselves better and, in turn, those around us. By following our personal resonance and speaking our Truth, we'll also find our life becomes easier and more enjoyable.

Because no one else has the answers to how to live our life apart from us, by allowing our inner being to guide us, we allow the positive change we want to see manifest. And with it we can soar, for ascension is less about what we know and more about integrating who we are by accepting all aspects of our being, including our strengths, setbacks, shadows and successes.

For eons, humanity hasn't enjoyed personal empowerment owing to the collective sense of unworthiness. On the surface, this may appear as procrastination, but the root cause lies far deeper. When we choose to unite with our Self (or with our twin soul as represented by another person), we're choosing to heal our internal wounds that are associated with the masculine and feminine aspects of Creation, i.e. the perceived hurt our soul felt when it originally separated from Source to live a physical experience. Although we can never be 'separate' from Source, if the wounded masculine could be encapsulated into a belief, it would be: 'The world is not enough.' Likewise, the wounded feminine would believe: 'I am not enough.' Both beliefs are distorted stories of scarcity that we've carried for too long and can transform when we choose to rise.

Using the 'life movie' metaphor, our stories of lack may manifest as not feeling worthy of getting up and leaving a movie we're not enjoying. Instead, we may sit there because we feel we *should*, or we're too comfy or idle to move, or we're too busy criticizing or blaming the world for what we're seeing. We may moan about our life, saying things like 'I'm sick of this relationship', I'm sick of being overweight', 'I'm sick of being broke', but it's not until we become sick and tired of being sick and tired that we'll be inspired to change the picture. At this breakthrough point, positive change can flow in as we take our creative attention to where we wish to be.

Loving Your Mind

Because we're all born with the same potential, whether we create change or stay the same rests on our beliefs.

A belief is a consistent thought our mind replays and if we're not aware of it, we will act and create from that belief on a subconscious level. Therefore, the quickest and most effective way to create the change we want and bring endless joy to our life is to be conscious of our beliefs. That way, we can dictate our choices.

Since working with the unicorns, on the last day of each month I'll take an hour out to 'sift' through my beliefs. I'll check in with the viewpoints my subconscious is replaying about each area of my life and how I relate to the world. I'll try them on like clothes to see if they still fit me. Those I've borrowed from others or that are tattered and doing nothing for my wellbeing, I'll let go, giving them to Source to recycle. And, as with any wardrobe, there are always a few sentimental pieces (stuffed right at the back!) from earlier in my life, or being kept for some future scenario, even though I know only too well they don't suit me. These are often the beliefs that are holding me back from allowing in the new. And so I'll sit and *wear* my beliefs, checking in with brazen honesty to see if they suit me or not.

◊ Mental Spring-Cleaning ◊

Sifting through your beliefs and principles is spring cleaning for the mind, a way of clearing out the old programmes that have been automatically controlling your life to make room for the magical unknown to enter.

Clear Mind

Unicorns highlight the importance of staying fluid in your beliefs, of never assuming anything without personal exploration. Truth is not fixed – it evolves as your perspective shifts.

Likewise, what you believe is what you'll receive from Creation. For example, the reality of your bank balance will reflect your beliefs concerning money, either its lack or its flow. Saying an affirmation each morning to increase your abundance won't work if you're countering this with opposing beliefs throughout your day. To receive clearly, think clearly. Be mindful of your mind and heartful of your soul, and the universe will deliver to you accordingly.

◊   To gain the most out of this exercise, first follow the Four Essential Steps (pages 78–82) and then sense

your third eye unicorn horn fully illuminating so you
can have a clear, loving Source perspective.

◊ Close your eyes and feel into the areas of your life
that you wish to spring-clean – your health, home life,
relationships, contribution to the world and so on.

◊ One by one, look at the beliefs you're carrying about
these areas. Ask yourself, 'Do I believe [e.g. I need to
work so hard] because my personal experience has led
me to accept this as my Truth or is this something I've
been conditioned to believe by others?'

◊ Keep the views that feel true and still of value, and
recycle those that don't by giving them to Source with
thanks for everything this energy has supported you
with.

◊ Use this question to bring Light to other beliefs until
you feel you've refined your Truth enough for the time
being.

◊ Repeat this process on a regular basis to keep mind,
heart and soul wholly and solely connected to your
Truth.

NB: It's often the beliefs – and their associated emotional
charge – we've adopted from those we love the most that
are the stickiest and therefore the hardest to strip away. For
instance, it took me a few rounds of this exercise to liberate
the guilt behind the belief 'I shouldn't leave food on my plate'
after years of my gran saying how wasteful and disrespectful
it was to leave food. So, keep persevering with compassion

for all concerned, trusting you're not dishonouring your loved ones by choosing your own perspective. Let yourself be empty so you can be full of God, knowing always it's safe and right to be your own person, your sincere Self.

◊ ◊ ◊ ◊

Loving Your Heart

After separating from Jonathan and healing my timeline through the *12 Days of Love* meditations, I realized how much I'd bought into the beliefs of others, including limiting 'spiritual' philosophies, and how much these had been hindering me from being my Self. Sifting through my values helped me to see the world through clear eyes and not the co-dependent filter I'd also created. This made it easier to hear my soul, which was guiding me to certify teachers in the UK in Angel Healing® and Atlantean Crystal Healing™ so that I could take the courses around America. Both modalities were asking to be shared globally.

So, after training additional teachers, I closed Ethereal Light, gave up the lease on my flat and shed all my material possessions. It felt fitting to clear my physical space to fully embrace a new chapter. I headed first to Portland, Maine, a city the unicorns had repeatedly encouraged me, through signs and synchronicities, to explore for my personal growth. My guides appreciated the emotional roller coaster I'd been on and how much energy had been put into advancing the therapy systems; now was time to let myself rest, play and integrate all that would unfold.

I could fill a few books over, beautiful soul, with the many magical experiences the States saw fit to grace me with, from meeting soul family to becoming friends with enlightened masters who could materialize Light from their fingertips and change the weather at will, to having experiences with the Knights Templar, incarnated elementals, Mary Magdalene and Merlin, among more earthly connections. However, my most profound experience was learning how limitless Love could be through healing and expanding my sexuality in a way that was reflected by those who were open and fluid in their relationships. By allowing my stance on romantic love to be brought to Light, I realized how much we all search for the feelings we enjoyed when we were first in love, whether those feelings were acceptance, connection, freedom, security and so on, and irrespective of how old we were when we fell in love.

For example, think about the first person you fell into romantic love with. If you could encapsulate the feeling of this relationship into one enjoyable emotion, what would it be? When (if) this relationship ended, think about the central reason for that separation and how you felt at this juncture. Through my personal experience and service to others, I believe the crux to all immobilizations in our life stem from how we felt in the latter moment – the moment we first believed we'd lost love and, in turn, our personal power. Because our soul is always striving for unity, we may try to restore this perceived lack by eating, drinking or abusing ourselves through subconscious beliefs and behaviour. Or we may look to others to fulfil us. All the while forgetting we have within us everything we need to feel full...

I first fell in love at the age of 12 and being with that soul suffused me with a great sense of fun. I didn't want to end our relationship, but succumbed to peer pressure. As I grew up, fun was my primary intention in every pursuit and subsequent relationships, and my Achilles' heel was yielding to the requests of others, which took the *fun* out of everything! The open-hearted souls I met in the States reflected what the unicorns had already shared with me – never limit or label Love, just be authentic and all you seek will find you. In order to let fun flow anew in my life, I had to forgive myself for ending my younger relationship and thereby lift the counter pattern of people-pleasing.

I'm sharing this story to support you in reclaiming any lost joys from your first physical memory of being in love, which will parallel the feeling of being unified with Source and the illusion of separation that can be felt with choosing to live a physical life. When we understand our life *is* living as Love, we not only heal and empower ourselves, but we also feel fulfilled by who we are, where we are and whom we are with.

As I reclaimed my fun, the courage came to step fully onto my path as a writer and teacher of ascension. And, as I would discover when returning home to Scotland, to become a mother, too.

#RisingReflections

- *'Would it benefit me to enjoy more of the feeling I felt when I was first in love?'*
- *'What needs to happen to allow more of this joy into my life?'*

Loving Your Body

While living in the States, I contracted Lyme disease, an infection caused by a bacterium carried on ticks. I'd learned from meeting gnomes (earthly elemental beings) via my KittySoaps journey to stay rational and grounded in times of ill health. They'd said that disease states manifested physically when we were out of alignment with our vibration, meaning illness is our body's way of healing/returning to our Self. It's only when we're too focused on our physical symptoms – which are in truth indicators from our body's intelligence that we're out of alignment – that we perpetuate the dis-ease state more.

Earth elementals also guide us never to identify with dis-ease states by saying, for example, 'I have Lyme disease' or 'I am a sufferer of...', either to ourselves or in conversations. This is to allow the symptoms (and their story) to drop out of our awareness so our body can return to its natural state of wellbeing.

Coming from a scientific background, it took me a while to trust this 'simplistic' way of looking at 'illness', yet it made perfect sense and has served me every time I've been unwell or come out of alignment.

Although most of humanity still reaches for pharmaceuticals to treat symptoms of misalignment, many souls are realizing that by tuning into the consciousness of their ailments first, they can restore their health without external soothing. Elementals and unicorns are holding this vision high, so we can learn to honour our body's intelligence in showing us what needs to be rebalanced in our beliefs and behaviour to enjoy better health. This can be facilitated by asking what you're experiencing, whether it's the flu, a headache or cancer, to join you in a heart-to-heart conversation. By giving your body a chance to speak and be heard in this way, you're supporting any discomfort to merge back into the Love of who you are.

◊ From Dis-ease to Ease ◊

◊   If you feel disempowered by a current dis-ease state, take a few moments to close your eyes and come into relaxed awareness.

◊   Bring your focus to where you feel the discomfort stems from within/around your body and then let yourself breathe deeply into this area.

◊   Speak to the discomfort by saying, 'I am here and I am listening. Do you have a message for me?'

◊   Sense any subtle or direct messages that come to you

now. Try not to force this to happen, just allow this part of your body to respond in its own way.

◊ Although sensations of discomfort may have lessened by now, thank this part of you for sharing and then ask, 'What would support your full return to health?'

◊ You may receive a list of inspired action steps, lifestyle changes, practices and/or medicines to apply, or you may receive a singular focus to restore vibrancy, such as to increase self-care. Listen with an open heart and soul to what can best support you and your body to enjoy a more cohesive, loving relationship.

◊   ◊   ◊   ◊

#RisingReflection

• *'Listening to my body, I realize I can improve its health and vibrancy by...'*

Integrating Your Soul

When we embrace the quest of soul embodiment, everything in our life becomes synchronistic as if Creation were a puppeteer orchestrating our life in the most mystical, magical and often most mischievous of ways!

Tuning into Lyme disease, I first felt the drag of the symptoms and their on-the-surface effect of disempowering my physical body. But diving deeper, the underlying message and medicine of this consciousness was encouraging me to become empowered. At the same time, I was finding my flow with fun again, and embracing my path as a writer and teacher. Both my body and soul were showing me that it was time to step up and shine. Shifting my perspective on Lyme disease and the events of my past enabled me to respect my physical self as much as I honoured my creative Self. It also enabled me to better understand that empowerment flows – and feels natural – when we choose to live in conscious union with all that we are.

After taking the time to listen to my body and soul, I was then inspired to return to my childhood home of Blairgowrie in Scotland. Just as I was getting comfortable teaching my therapy systems, including Unicorn Healing®, which more people felt ready for after the 11-11-11 shift into the Aquarian Age, my soul brought back into my life my teenage boyfriend Greg, who'd never left my awareness over the years. He'd always been the 'one that got away' and it felt as though Creation were giving us another chance to be together. Soon after, Greg and I rekindled our relationship and eventually moved in together, following the incessant yet charming prompts of his son, Jack, who wanted his dad to be happy following his divorce. After releasing the sense of 'needing' a partner, I found myself emotionally free for one and, for the first time in my life, free in my sexuality, too, devoid of the shame and fear of past abusive stories.

I continued to write and teach, while studying to become a Kundalini Yoga teacher. This ancient 'yoga of awareness' helped me to heal following Lyme disease. I especially enjoyed the meditative tantra aspect because of its focus on merging the self and Self as One.

Wanting to understand more about tantra, I began researching teaching courses and discovered something called a vision quest. Reading about this Native American ceremony created truth bumps all over my body! And Hethgar was nudging me forward, indicating that this was the next part of my journey.

Vision Quest

> 'We are Earth people on a spiritual journey to
> the stars. Our quest, our Earth walk, is to look within,
> to know who we are, to see that we are connected
> to all things, that there is no separation, only in
> the mind.'
>
> **LAKOTA SEER**

This poignant quote sums up what I learned through one of the oldest, most profound rites of passage, a vision quest – a ceremony that gives you a wider sense of who you are in every way. It's something I recommend you experience (with a quest leader) if you haven't already.

Vision Quest

During Hurricane Bertha in 2014 – one of the wettest and wildest storms to hit the UK – I stepped across a spiritual threshold, held by my esteemed shamanic leader, David Wendl-Berry, to learn and listen from my soul as reflected by nature. While he and his trainee remained at base camp, for four days and nights my quest journey was to live nearby in an isolated part of the raw Cairngorm mountains of northern Scotland. I intentionally had no tent, no food and nothing to distract me from the vision my soul wanted to share. This was a time to face my inner shadows and allow my deepest Truth to emerge.

The land I'd chosen to be my quest home was filled with silver birch trees and the presence of unicorns was made even more palpable by my intention to live purely in the Spirit realm for the duration of my stay. There were many elemental beings, Highland cattle and deer roaming freely. I was in their world now and I hoped they'd support me with the aim of my quest – to integrate my Truth and live it fully. But, as with most people on a vision quest, my soul had led me there for another reason. This was also my rite of passage to become a mother.

As ceremony is the language you use to dial into the Spirit world, I was given specific ceremonies to do each day to help me to decode what nature was mirroring. The unicorns and the spirits of the land assisted in most of them, especially in my 'deathlodge' – a sacred circle of empowerment you create and sit within on the first night of your quest. In a deathlodge, you affirm that it's your last night on Earth and before you die you're calling in the spirits (physical or not) with whom you've unfinished business, in order to clear any conflicts. I had so much baggage to release, it took three separate deathlodges to release fully what was ready to go!

In the ceremony, I called in people to face, then energies like self-sabotage to address and then asked to face the darkness itself to witness what the core beliefs of my internal shadows were. This 'spirit of darkness' was who I needed to face the most and the pitch-black terrain of the raw Scottish landscape was the perfect place to do so. Steadily, and with all the courage I could muster, I broke down the barriers of self-created fear. And because the darkness itself was supporting this ceremony, it reflected to me its incredible service in helping us to comprehend our own power, as well as being the creative space for birthing the new. As Light was shed on my inner shadows, I began to feel safe and realized that 'darkness' was just another form of Light, another form of Source supporting us in being who we came here to be.

As understanding flooded into my consciousness, my associated fears of the unknown began to diminish. My power was being reclaimed. At that moment, I grasped how much a vision quest (and our earthly life quest) connects us to our divine potential, which is forever neutral in its vibration, meaning it rests on us whether we create a more positive- or negative-seeming life. The unicorns had reflected this Truth to me and nature was now doing the same, but in a more physical way. Both allies were bringing the message that we can integrate our fears into Love, our ego into soul and our self into Self, as well as carry out anything else we have chosen to do in this unique human experience.

My next lesson was how to combine being a spiritual teacher who to all intents and purposes lived mostly in celestial realms with becoming a mother, something that would require me to be more grounded in my body than ever before.

It was on the evening of returning from the vision quest that this understanding began to blossom. For Rowan's soul appeared in my awareness with a gentleness that said, 'I'm ready.'

When Jonathan had exited my life, I thought the possibility of Rowan coming into my life had gone, too, yet Rowan had been very present throughout my quest journey and had felt more than happy for Greg to be the earthly father. When I shared the presence of Rowan's soul with Greg, he said he was ready, too, albeit a little amazed as well, as he wasn't as attuned to perceiving Spirit. Yet, he did feel the conscious co-creation of Rowan, which, to date, has been the most divinely grounded experience of my life.

The next day, still enchanted by the quest's magic and the ineffable experience of Rowan's soul flowing through us, I enjoyed the sense of possibly being pregnant. From a physical perspective, fasting for nearly five days wasn't conducive to conception, yet the quest had re-emphasized that anything was possible!

As soon as Greg arrived home with Jack that evening, I felt an impulse for us to go for a walk. He suggested a trail, but as we drove there, we stumbled upon a forest we hadn't visited before. 'Let's get out here,' I said, feeling Mother Earth speak through me.

The boys went in one direction and I let my feet walk where they wanted to go. And then I saw it – a forest of rowan trees!

A grandmother-like tree beckoned me to her. Having learned how to communicate with trees on my quest, I sat down to listen to her sage counsel.

She said, 'Take these,' directing me to a fallen bunch of rowan berries. 'Keep them by your bed and near you as you give birth.'

Then it was as if the canopy of the entire forest gathered together to envelop me in a heartfelt embrace. The warmth of this still moves me to this day. The trees were blessing me and the beautiful soul who, by their account, was going to be there soon!

A few weeks later, it was confirmed: I was pregnant with Rowan. And to my surprise, Rowan's soul took the form of a boy, not a girl, as I had been shown years earlier. He still had blond curly hair and a knowing, mischievous manner, but he chose to manifest as male in gender to support the new path I was on and the one that he'd chosen for himself with Greg as his father.

A Soul's Guide to Being Human

Sometimes we need to ask ourselves who we are without our spiritually in order to find our humanity. For to embody our soul is *to integrate all that we are*. This was something that manifested on my vision quest with the help of Rowan's soul and my inner child, Catriona, the name I was given at birth. The angels gave me the name 'Calista' when I left science and embraced my spiritual path, and even though it felt so natural to embrace that name, the quest showed me that not going by my original name meant I was cutting myself off from a part of myself that symbolized my humanity. To become a mother, I needed to find, reclaim and unify with my younger physical self, which the vision quest gave me the chance to do.

As a mother now, I appreciate how wonderful it is to be a spiritual teacher helping others to merge with their divinity. But the personal mastery is how to maintain the same grace while changing nappies, functioning with little sleep and undertaking the many other 'training courses' from the earthly school of motherhood.

Unicorn Mother and Baby

Many awakened people want to become spiritual to retreat from life, but the real joy is *advancing* through life, through all its facets, including fear, contrasts and day-to-day mundanity, and still be connected to who you are. That is the path of mastery, the path that unicorns are here to help us to live. They envisage us being able to radiate our authentic Love in all situations, treating every person in the same way and seeing every aspect of life as equally exquisite. Granted, we'll have our off-days, but these are just our 'growing days', when we're refining ourselves even more.

Stop Being Everyone to Others and Be Wholly Your Self

I lived this lesson the hard way through aligning to hypothyroidism and postnatal depression following the birth of Rowan. Despite knowing these dis-ease states were a product of misalignment and that I was equipped to bring myself back into balance, often I just didn't want to wake up in the morning. I'd manifested all these incredible blessings in my life yet was looking for the escape route.

The reason life felt so challenging was because I was separating from myself. I had lost touch with who I was in trying to be the perfect partner, the perfect mum, and the perfect cook and housekeeper. And throughout my maternity leave I continued to teach, despite promising myself I wouldn't. I clung to the illusionary notion I could do all and be it all, but eventually something had to break, and that something was me. Depression descended, but although those were dark days, my unicorn guides were ever-present. They reminded me to look beyond the different labels I was putting on myself to stop the sense of feeling split in my energy. Ultimately, this meant I had to stop trying to be everything for everyone and instead be wholly me for me, first and foremost – a trap many of us fall into, whether we're a parent or not.

Trusting this sage guidance from the unicorns and the reflection of their Light in conversations with friends, I began to leverage myself out of depression, realizing I could still be my authentic Self and live my Truth irrespective of what *hat* I was wearing.

Adjusting from living in the 5D world as a spiritual teacher to becoming a mother was challenging only because I was treating both worlds as separate. My lesson was to integrate my reality so no matter whether I was changing nappies, cooking dinner or attuning souls to higher-dimensional beings, I was allowing myself to be fully my Self. This valuable lesson is one for which I'm most grateful.

Unicorns would like us all to realize that we're multi-dimensional beings who, despite the many hats we feel we wear in one day, can always choose to be true to our Selves. This process takes surrendering and incorporating every aspect of ourselves into our 'now' moment. But it is a process that ultimately leads us to live a happier, more balanced life. In addition, as we adjust to knowing we're a multi-dimensional being, we realize that the multiple roles we've chosen to experience (and identify with) is the uniqueness that makes us who we are.

By facing and accepting my inner shadows, I found myself again and steadily understood the steps needed to move fully out of depression and back into joy. Light was once again found in the darkness, with the salient reminder to see Love in all, from a rainbow to a muddy puddle, for Creation is forever present. Moreover, the more understanding and compassion we bring to the human experience we're having, the closer we become to Source and ultimately to living as Source.

Accepting Your Shadows

Just as we have a progressive higher Self, we also have a seemingly regressive counterpart, the shadow self. The great psychologist Carl Jung maintained the shadow side represented everything we weren't fully conscious of or an unconscious aspect of our personality that our conscious ego didn't recognize. As we tend to reject the least desirable aspects of our personality, the shadow side is deemed to be negative. Yet, there's much to be gained from delving into our shadow – like Truth and unending creativity.

Integrating our shadow side leads to self-actualization just as surely as accepting we're a divine being does, for both paths bring about positive transformation. And the more we're aware of our shadow side, the lighter it is. Conversely, the less embodied it is, the denser it is.

Our shadow side is comprised of the parts of our being that judge ourselves and others and hold us back from doing certain things we know we'd enjoy. Until we integrate our shadow traits, we project them onto others and if we're not aware of this, it's easy to fuel discord with those around us, which only widens the gap between where we are and living the joy of a balanced life.

Unicorns tell us that our shadow is no less worthy of love and acceptance than our Light, for in truth we have a golden shadow side, too. While the seemingly darker shadow side asks to be integrated, the golden side asks to be expressed, for it represents all the talents, skills, dreams and beauty that we consciously or subconsciously diminish, deny, refuse to develop or fear to show.

You may be like other beautiful souls who are masters at minimizing their inner gold, yet by integrating your denser shadows, you can know what you're good at and step more into it. And as you keep expressing your talents, you accrue more and suddenly what feels like a pipe dream can become your everyday physical reality.

Remember, your soul wants you to *live* your dreams, not to withhold them for fear you're not good enough to shine or that someone will judge you for it. Let your Light dissolve those denser fears and use their grit to become a golden pearl who shines out, seen, heard and in every way empowered by Love. Let your life be the Love you give and the message you take into the world.

◊ Regaining Balance ◊

We are living in a time of great awareness where, no matter what route they take, our shadows are coming forward to be acknowledged and integrated. Perhaps you've doubts about yourself and how others view you. Or maybe you doubt the path you're on, your connection with your Self and your contribution to the world. To some extent, we're all going through the motions of personal acceptance and integration, for this is the primary lesson here in Earth School.

For a moment, bring to your awareness a current conflict in your life. Could this conflict be mirroring an aspect of yourself that you haven't acknowledged or accepted yet? When we start to acknowledge our shadow side, we may not like what we see and even deny the regressive aspects, especially if they appear in the guise of cowardice, egotism or self-doubt. Others may see them in our personality, but we may fear the consequence of shining awareness onto them. The road of spiritual understanding really isn't for the faint-hearted, but for the intrepid among us, the rewards of self-realization are Infinite!

◊   For this exercise, come into a state of relaxed awareness and call in your unicorn guides.

◊   Intend that your heart unicorn horn is fully illuminated as it spirals to Creation, both outwardly and inwardly.

◊   Ask Source to show you the shadows you're carrying, i.e. the judgements, fears and doubts you're ready to face, by asking:

'Loving Source, what shadows exist within me that have the potential to birth new understanding? I acknowledge and integrate them and come into balance now.

Thank you. And so it is.'

◊ Witness the energetic integration of each shadow
    sense as it flows to you and is in-lightened in you.

◊ And then repeat this process as you ask:

> *'Loving Source, what Light exists within me that*
> *needs to be nurtured to birth new understanding?*
> *I acknowledge and express it and come into balance now.*
>
> *Thank you. And so it is.'*

◊ Witness the energetic integration of each shadow
    sense as it flows to you and is in-lightened in you.

◊ Thank Source and your unicorn guides for holding
    the space for these loving shifts to take place.

Repeat this exercise often to keep grounded, balanced and
radiant as you continue to rise and shine.

If you'd prefer to see your inner shadows and gold, before
going to sleep, ask your consciousness to bring these aspects
into your dreams so you can face and integrate them. Call
on your unicorn guides to amplify this experience so
you're fully conscious of everything and can write all that
happened down in your journal when you wake. Tracking
your journey of self-realization will help you to unleash
your untapped potential and your experiences (when
shared) will be likely to help others, too.

◊ ◊ ◊ ◊

#RisingReflections

- *'By integrating my shadow side, I grow with renewed courage and...'*

- *'By expressing my golden side, I feel happier within myself and...'*

Rise and Shine

Chapter 8
Rainbow Rising

B efore physical life, we're pure Love. There's nothing to transform, we simply *are*. Then, through a conscious decision to experience Love through a physical filter, we come into being in this life. Until we know we're on a journey of exploration, we can overlook our divinity, yet we still feel that desire to spread our wings and move life forward. From a physical-only perspective, this drive can be misconstrued as a need to acquire things, achieve goals and be someone based on an external framework. But when this sleepy misinterpretation is shaken away, we encounter our Self and our conscious mind begins to blend personal desires with a question that develops as our consciousness does: 'How can I best serve Love?'

This sincere enquiry doesn't mean we have to surrender the joy of being human to serve an external God, but asks how we can best partner our humanity to live boldly and love wholly *as* God. By letting this be our experience, we can make life juicer by taking it beyond its perceived limits, all the while appreciating that the pilgrimage of life is the path on which all the gems of Creation are found.

The importance of this revelation was reiterated by my daily walks in nature whilst writing *Unicorn Rising*. Because unicorns are closely related to Gaia, the magic of the natural world asked to be woven into the pages, too. During my walks, nature showed that she isn't every season in one day (albeit in Scotland it can often feel like that!), but there are gifts and beauty in all her cycles, just as there are in every moment of our lifetime. Equally, nature never rushes or judges, only moves with the same cosmic ebb and flow as we do, forever trusting that Love will find a way.

While nature and unicorns both support us in having a smooth ascent back into Love, they also highlight the importance of becoming comfortable with allowing the unknown to become known along the way. For our path and purpose are never fixed into a bullet-pointed list of experiences and assignments – we have the delicious freedom to craft them for ourselves through our Creative will. Our soul, and the nudges from our spiritual senses and guidance team, can show us the way, but it's up to us to fill in the details – and allow them to fill themselves in sometimes. By accepting this, we'll instinctively know when to allow life to flow through its divine intelligence and when to take inspired action. In other words, we'll know when to *inhale* and *exhale* life, just as we do with our breath, to create the change that's most important to us.

By listening and allowing the subtlety of your inner magic to light the way, you may find you'll have more energy, too, for the sense of having to control life or the feeling you must fight or struggle to be happy will disappear. As Source guides, nothing that's for you, and *is* you, will go past you, so enjoy being in the moment you're in.

And if fear still creeps in, face that fear and rise, friend. Be okay with spreading your wings and rising up out of your comfort zone, knowing Creation is bringing you the fulfilment you've asked for, that you're equipped to receive and deserve to have.

You were Born to Rise

I believe we're all 'ascension pioneers', a term more fitting than the more common label of 'lightworker', given that the Aquarian Age is the era of expanding consciousness. According to unicorns, there's nothing truly to 'work' at in this *human and being* life experience – all we have to do is in-joy and create!

Likewise, our celestial friends share that it's time to say with confidence, 'I created that!' To affirm we are Creators takes responsibility, but it also empowers us to ignite more positive change. This isn't about personal ego, it's about affirming we are an embodied soul co-creating with Source, who's within us and reflected back to us by those around us. If what we're creating fails, that's okay – mastery lies in the attempt and in the tenacity to keep advancing. For our gifts are too precious to withhold and our Love too bright to be denied.

This was the learning through limitation that our soul acquired in the last Piscean Age, but now those fish have found a new flow and we are ready to learn through expansion.

As we learn to swim within the Aquarian pool, we encounter other souls on the same journey. By supporting one another, we automatically open the door of unity consciousness for all to enjoy. For our hearts and souls are forever communicating with one another, as they are with nature, our guides, ancestors and all life. This makes us a family within the school of Mother Earth and even though we all have unique lessons of Love, together we can create a brighter world.

Do you feel an inner call to support the Earth? As an ascension pioneer, you carry the template for the new Golden Age within your consciousness – a positive shift that is born through you by being your Self and sharing your gifts with the world. And whatever contribution you're inspired to make, do so with a full heart, without need of recognition or reward. Share, invent, collaborate and aid simply because it feels good to live from your soul and draw on your individuality. While there will always be polarity within physical life, by learning to accept contrast and to respect others' gifts and differences, you will find that everyone benefits. Your mind becomes free-thinking, your heart becomes full of unconditional Love, and your spirit inspires change through positive action and example.

Co-creating a New Earth

If we show up to give to the world, our soul will connect to unicorns and other spiritual helpers who wish to support our global contribution. Partnering such luminaries is an act of divine magic, healing and wholeness, and the bond is a sacred one to cherish.

Through helping many people to connect to their spirit guides, I've witnessed the tendency of some to focus solely on what they can personally gain. I've also realized that many view their relationship with Spirit through a utilitarian filter, i.e. they ask their guides for constant help. While our non-physical friends *are* willing to assist us, we must treat them with the love and respect we'd like to receive. We can encourage this to happen by creating a stronger resonance with them and focusing more on our shared purpose: to create a brighter world. Asking our guides, 'How can I best contribute to the world through our alliance?', or 'What's your highest vision for the ascension of humanity and the Earth?', or 'How can I share your blessings with the world?' is a great place to start.

Our spiritual guides – who, you'll remember, are a team comprised of at least 11 ethereal helpers at any given time – can bring to our awareness the knowing of their divine purpose for assisting the world to ascend. Contributing our love, time and energy to that purpose is especially welcomed and honoured.

By choosing this path, we may find ourselves asking questions that take us beyond personal desires and into the realm of creative curiosity – questions such as: 'How can I bless this environment?', or 'How can I bring greater kindness into the world?', or 'How can I assist in birthing the new Golden Age?' Whatever response we receive, and whatever creations we develop with our guides, we should aim to share them openly rather than letting this energy sit within us. By staying unattached to everything we give and receive, we honour the thread of sovereignty that aligns us with our guides and with the rest of the world, for we're all drawing on the same universal Source.

If we keep up regular communication with our guides, our vibration will also continue to rise and shine. For example, many of us haven't connected to the Light of the unicorns before, and so it will take time for us to hold their Light and to channel their frequency to benefit others.

Let the Light of your guides steadily become part of your wholeness as you co-create a more loving, co-operative world.

Earth Healing with the Sidhe

For a long time, spiritual self-help books have focused on how to blend our consciousness with that of angels and ascended masters, so we may know our divinity. Now, the natural world is reaching out to support us in living our humanity, with unicorns acting as the bridge to help us to enjoy life as an embodied soul.

Unicorn World Healing

Whilst I was writing this chapter, different types of nature spirits visited me, sharing how we can partner the planet through *encountering* nature. For example, if you saw a tree, you might consider its form and feel its energy, but if you were to *encounter* it, you would meet its soul and allow (if it agreed) your energies to synch so that you would *know* each other. This is how a tree meets our consciousness: it doesn't see you or me, for example, it sees only our vibration and intent to communicate with it.

The elemental beings who can teach us the most about encountering nature are the *Sidhe*, the ancient faery souls, sometimes referred to as 'the shining ones' or 'the hidden ones', who live within the Earth. Hethgar has a strong Celtic connection with the *Sidhe* and together they gifted this simple but effective way of bringing loving empowerment to the planet. Although Gaia is adept at raising her consciousness, we can energetically support her by in-lightening the destruction on and around her, so she may enjoy a more graceful ascent.

◊ Earth Healing with the *Sidhe* ◊

When you're ready, please prepare yourself with the 'Rise and Shine' meditation (page 16) before enjoying the following...

> In a relaxed state of awareness, bring your attention up and through your spiralling third eye unicorn horn. Sense you're sitting in a sacred stone circle. You can feel the earth below you and the sun above you, and hear the sound of water gently flowing nearby.

> There's a soft rush of wind through the trees as your unicorn guides come to greet you. They tell you this is the meeting place of the Sidhe, your primal cousins who wish to assist you to form a closer connection with Mother Earth.

Send out a call from your heart to ask for your guardian Sidhe to come forward. Breathe deeply and slowly as this loving soul enters your awareness.

For a moment, enjoy just being together. Let yourself gently attune to each other's vibration as you get to know them.

Your guide invites you to send healing to the planet by visualizing the Earth as a spinning orb in front of you. Open your heart to all that is Mother Earth, intending and sensing that you're bathing the world in luminous Love now.

As you project your blessings out to the world, the Sidhe are radiating their Love from within the planet. And joining in this sacred healing are many unicorns, directing their horns of Light to the world and assisting those who are ready to awaken their consciousness to do so with grace and ease.

Keep sending your Love for as long as you're guided to do so, asking Mother Earth, 'Is there anything else I can do to support your highest wellbeing?'

Listen to what Gaia shares and follow any inspired action steps that may come to you now or later.

When you're ready, gently bring your awareness back into your body, thanking all concerned and drinking some water to ground yourself.

◈ ◈ ◈ ◈

#RisingReflections

- *'Meeting my Sidhe guide and blessing the world together was significant because...'*
- *'I can give Love to the planet in this way and also by...'*

Encountering Pegasians

After Rowan was born, my contribution to Mother Earth came in the form of making Unicorn Healing® an online modality. I was apprehensive about how such a practical course could be made into a remote learning programme, but it manifested perfectly, just as Hethgar had said it would, and attracted ascension pioneers from all over the world. Our community remains, to this day, the most real, loving and non-judgemental of spaces – but I wouldn't expect anything less from those who're living the magical Love and Truth of their soul!

One day in 2015, as I was passing on a unicorn attunement to a new student, a Pegasus appeared. Pegasians are winged horses who are closely related to unicorns. I'd worked with them in a meditation class at Ethereal Light, but they'd never manifested to me during an attunement. Afterwards, my student said they'd witnessed our surprise guest, too, and I wondered if the visitation had been solely for their path or if it was connected to developing the system.

When I attuned the next group of students, everyone had a personal Pegasian guide appear! From that point on, these divine allies joined Unicorn Healing® and they have since supported profound transformations in the lives of those linked to the programme.

While I was encountering Pegasians in my work, their Light was manifesting in my personal life, too. With training students, nursing Rowan and healing my body, I hadn't realized I was pregnant again! It wasn't until my physiotherapist, who was treating what my doctor believed was a split in my abdominal muscles, saw my swollen stomach and said, 'Are you *sure* you're not pregnant?' that I discovered I was.

When I was driving to the hospital for my first scan, there were rainbow clouds all over the sky. From a scientific perspective, these rare iridescent clouds are produced when tiny ice crystals or water droplets in the air cause sunlight to diffract, creating a rainbow-like effect. This was the first time I'd seen rainbow clouds so palpably vibrant – they were alive, and much more than water and ice crystals was coming through to me!

Guided to stop the car, I had an overwhelming sense of the Pegasians' presence being reflected through the clouds, announcing that the little soul I was carrying was connected to them. Tuning in more intently to this, I realized the energy I was seeing was the *same* Light I felt within me. At that moment, the realization dawned that I wasn't just bringing another soul through my body, I was giving birth to a new world, an *Eden*, which was the very name my son chose to be called.

While carrying Eden, I found myself listening to motivational speakers like Tony Robbins and Les Brown, and reading inspiring books like Baird T. Spalding's *Life and Teaching of the Masters of the Far East*. I could sense the Pegasians reminding me of my Infinite capabilities after I'd spent months stifled by the weight of postnatal depression and hypothyroidism. Likewise Eden, ever the Pegasian soul, was urging me to believe in myself and let go of the disabling beliefs that were still replaying in my mind, such as the feeling I couldn't live my dreams now that I was a mother. Although I had a toolbox full of ways to come back into alignment, I was being shown my self-created limitations and the inspired means to break them down – a kindness that reminded me that even when we're at our lowest ebb, Creation flows in and carries us to where we want to be.

What are the Gifts of the Pegasians?

Pegasians are often associated with the angelic realm because of their wings, yet they can also manifest with a unicorn horn. Whereas unicorns reflect our soul, and the knowing and embodiment of our path, power and purpose, Pegasians reflect the potential of our soul to rise and keep rising in any direction we wish to go – they are the ultimate inspirational coaches!

You may have felt a Pegasus with you in your unicorn attunement or perhaps you saw wings. Often, Pegasians act as an overlighting presence in support of the Light of the unicorns. For example, when I first connected with my

Pegasus guide, I saw their brilliant huge wings arc over my unicorn guides and me. It was a comforting image that illustrated how the unicorns and Pegasians work as One consciousness to support all concerned.

While unicorns are masters at helping us to stay aware, connected and receptive to Creation, Pegasians help us to plant creative seeds to grow our passions. This can make their energy feel faster and more refined than that of the unicorns. For example, after attuning to them (as you'll experience shortly), you may find yourself feeling more exuberant, with a diamond-like certainty that all you're focusing on will flourish.

Spread Your Wings

I've been blessed to experience this enlivened passion since encountering the Pegasians and you may feel it, too, from reading their 'Manifesto for a Better Life' – a passage they wrote through me in a time of weariness when I truly needed my butt kicked into action. Sometimes we need this type of bold loving to ignite a fire under our inertia and break us out of the cocoons we create.

Manifesto for a Better Life

There is a power within you so Great, so Magical and so ready to Rise. This greatness lives within your very breath, blood and bones, and now is the time to live it! Stand up, be seen, contribute your greatness and with your greatness see through life challenges for the opportunities they are to grow and be grown. When you stumble, curse the world or blame others for your situation. And if you feel lonely, lost or confused, reach inside yourself and say, 'I am worth more than this; I matter!' Understand these points of inception – welcome them. They are bearers of a clarity that would otherwise go unnoticed if you weren't strong enough to push through your limitations and fears. Embrace change. Keep believing in a greater You. A greater way to live. For this is your one opportunity to live this life. Enjoy it, express it and evolve it. Stand tall, divine soul. Cast off self-doubt. Let go of the validation, expectation and approval of others – the only person you need to prove yourself to is You. There's never judgement from Creation. There's never judgement from nature. There's never judgement from your soul and spirit team. The only one that judges is the self that puts things off, that puts you down, and that doesn't want You to break free. Give Love to that aspect and say, 'Come take my hand, beloved. Let's go on an adventure! Let's see what is on the other side. Let's see what magic we can create today. Rise with me!' It's time to say 'YES' and mean it. It's time to feel supported. To feel good. To feel here. For Creation is here. And all you need to do is look up and see yourself. All you need to do is look down and see yourself. All you need to do is look around and see yourself, and your creative potential. Let yourself be your Self. Don't live for tomorrows. For living for tomorrow is dying today. Don't be the person who dies full of dreams. Live your dreams. Live for today and say, 'Yes! I am here. I am awake. I am passionate for life. I am showing up for life, knowing I have what it takes to create, be or do anything. I am aligned. I am in the flow. I am ready to live and allow life's Infinite possibilities to flow through me like water, ever-changing, ever-vast, boundless, nameless, limitless and free. Free I am. Free like a unicorn, I live my path, express my purpose and stand in my power.

I am One with Creation. One with Life, I AM.

◊ Pegasus Attunement ◊

In this power-packed experience, you'll first meet your personal Pegasus guide, and then attune to their consciousness and the vibration they're gifting humanity – a stream of Source Light called the Diamond Ray. This consciousness is also called the Rainbow Ray, for the colours perceived in its Light are like those of the rainbow, but with many more colours, hues and crystalline variations that go beyond what our physical eyes can detect.

Receiving this attunement is receiving your full heart – all the Love and divine Light of Creation. As a result, you may feel that you begin to remember your celestial heritage, including other Golden Ages you've experienced, and awaken, at DNA level, your divine blueprint. And so, following your attunement, write down your experience in your journal while staying open and receptive to the positive transformation that may ensue.

When you attuned to the collective consciousness of the unicorns, you were given etheric horns of Light. Now you'll receive your wings! These natural extensions of your soul's highest expression can support you in fulfilling your highest potential whilst fully enjoying your earthly journey. Perhaps you've felt your wings before, if you've attuned to angels or worked alongside them. Pegasian wings assist in opening your heart (both front and back to give and receive), like angel wings do, but have the added benefit of keeping you open to your soul's multi-dimensional creative abilities.

Following your attunement, any time you visualize your wings opening, or have the intention that they should open, you're letting your soul fully express itself! Your confidence, courage and faith will grow as a result and you'll feel the breath of Creation beneath your wings supporting you in shining even more.

Pegasus Guide

As with angel wings, any time you wish to receive comfort, see your wings wrapping around you and feel the Love of the Creator holding you with the warming reassurance that you're loved, you're loveable and that you forever Love.

During your attunement, if you feel guided to move your body, flow with it, especially if you want to put your hands on parts of your body. And if you wish to lie down afterwards to help your body to acclimatize to the new energies, please do so.

When you're ready to receive, read through the journey below.

The attunement can take 20 minutes to an hour to receive, so it's best to give yourself plenty of time.

Please choose a comfortable place where you won't be disturbed and where you can sit upright comfortably. Rest your hands on your lap with your palms facing upwards. You may feel inspired to sit in nature or to imagine yourself there.

◊   Begin with the 'Rise and Shine' meditation (page 16).

◊   Then take a few moments before listening to/ reading your attunement. Breathe yourself into the moment and breathe out any questions, doubts or expectations, surrendering them to Source.

◊   Then, feeling centred, affirm aloud:

> *'I am ready to receive my attunement to the Pegasus*
> *realm and the frequency of the Diamond Ray and*
> *affirm that these gifts are perfect for me.*
> *I fully allow this Divine Light to align with me.*
>
> *Thank you. And so it is.'*

◊   Let go of feeling that you should be *doing* something
and enjoy this beautiful experience fully...

*Feeling yourself being held in the golden Light of Source,
take your attention up and through your third eye. Sense
your unicorn guides beside you, holding a high expansive
space in which your main Pegasus guide can join you
now.*

*Feel your heart open as you become aware of their
presence. You may sense their huge, luminous wings
and the wind they create both around and within you to
freshen and brighten your energy.*

*Open to what your guide looks like. Do they feel male/
female/of neutral vibration? Are they old or young? Do
they have a name? Get to know this beautiful soul as you
open to their Love.*

*Take your awareness to the centre of your back. Sense
your etheric wings. Feel them begin to unfold and unfurl
behind you as they emerge from your heart now. Fan
them out fully, and tune in to your sense of them and their
appearance. They are part of you – an extension of your
heart and soul.*

*It's safe to free your wings, to liberate yourself. There's
no need to shield yourself any more, for you are your
own protection. Let yourself be bare, bold and beautiful,
inhaling deeply all that you are and exhaling deeply
through your loving wings.*

A shining diamond now appears before you. It's clear enough to see through, yet vibrantly alive, filled with crystalline rainbow Light. It begins to spin in front of you, showing you all its sides and all its splendour.

On your next inhale, intend that the diamond moves into your heart. Sense it condensing down into luminous Light that penetrates every cell of your body, positively transforming and activating your DNA to vibrate in alignment with the cosmos and your divine blueprint. Feel yourself being switched on from the inside out. Breathe deeply and breathe fully as the Diamond Ray codes gently adjust to (and align with) your being.

If you're guided to do so, place your hands on a part of your being to receive healing. Let the Pegasian diamond Light move through you effortlessly. Receive whatever is best for you at this moment. Move your hands whenever you are guided and just enjoy this loving treatment. Know you're forever linked with Pegasians and may channel their energy for the highest wellbeing of all concerned. Whenever you need assistance to grow your dreams and passions, call on them.

Relax into this bliss.

When the energy begins to wane, give thanks to all concerned and for all the Love shared. Ground yourself by stretching out your body and drinking some water.

◊　◊　◊　◊

#RisingReflections

- 'Attuning to the consciousness of the Pegasians and the Diamond Ray is meaningful to me because...'

- 'Becoming one with this Light has instilled greater trust in...'

- 'I'll continue to partner my Pegasian guide for the purpose of...'

Unicorn Angel

Chapter 9
Unleash Your Magic – 30-Day Soul-Play!

You've experienced your childhood and your adulthood, now it's time to embody your Godhood! We teach children to play and we teach adults to work, but what does Godhood teach *us*? From a unicorn perspective, Godhood means to be, create, grow and share our whole Self. And what better way to unleash our inner magic than by turning the teachings shared throughout this book into a 30-day soul adventure?!

As part of the Unicorn Healing® programme, prospective practitioners are asked to complete a 30-day consecutive *sadhana* – a time to connect with their soul to deepen this most sacred of relationships. Through enjoying a daily spiritual practice, it becomes far easier to live life through our divine nature without cutting off our humanity in the process. And by showing up consistently for 30 days, we help our subconscious mind to reinforce the habit, so it becomes a lifelong commitment to our Self.

From witnessing the positive transformations of the Unicorn Healing® practitioners, I realized that what led them to connect to their soul the most – and brought about the greatest breakthroughs – was their 30-Day Soul-Play with their unicorn and Pegasian guides. You can read excerpts from the practitioners' *sadhana* journeys online at https://www.facebook.com/groups/unicornhealing. This is a private community page that you're welcome to join if you'd like to meet and share with those who've enjoyed, and are still enjoying, this adventure – aka your unicorn tribe!

Using Technology to Support Yourself

In this age of rising technology, we're drowning in information, yet hungry for wisdom. This makes a daily spiritual practice even more meaningful. It's important to give yourself this gift, for you can't experience your highest wellbeing if your spiritual wellbeing is low on your priority list. Over time, your *sadhana* will become a habit like other daily rituals: showering, eating, *sadhana*…

Technology can help you to stay with this if you use it to support yourself rather than distract yourself. Use it to enhance the human interaction of this adventure, i.e. by meeting kindred souls (perhaps even soul family) in the online unicorn tribe and exchanging experiences, ideas, tips and questions to build loving, supportive relationships. Remember, your vibe attracts your tribe and these days tribes gather on social media! As Edmund Lee astutely said, 'Surround yourself with the dreamers and the doers, the believers and the thinkers, but most of all, surround yourself with those who see the greatness within you, even when you don't see it yourself.'

You can also use technology to set an alarm to wake you, preferably before dawn, until getting up earlier becomes part of your automatic muscle memory.

What Does the 30-Day Soul-Play Entail?

In the Age of Aquarius, community is a powerful force we can lean into. By sharing with others, we understand that vulnerability is strength and connection bravery. For it takes courage to look at your life and say, 'I want more,' and even more courage to look at the world and say, 'I want to help.' The difference between those living a mediocre life and those enjoying an extraordinary existence is discipline, and consistency of discipline in committing to them Selves each day and never settling for less than what's possible.

To help you to find this courage and commitment, set aside the next 30 days and devote at least 20 minutes per day to inviting your unicorn and Pegasian guides to be consciously with you. Together, enjoy any of the meditations, exercises and reflective questions in this book or enjoy any other devotional theme you're inspired to expand upon, writing your experiences in your journal as you go.

The best time for a crystal-clear *sadhana* is before dawn. If this isn't possible for you, assign a time to which you can commit consistently. With having young children, I understand it's difficult to schedule in a shower some days, but by making your *sadhana* an absolutely non-negotiable sacred time for your Self, you will see that Love *will* find a way. And if you can only manage a few minutes of Source Breathing one day, that's okay, just be present and enjoy it.

◊ 30-Day Soul-Play ◊

Here are 30 ideas of what you could choose to focus on for each day of your soul-play. You'll invariably come up with your own, too, and that's great. If you feel they could benefit others, please share them with the online community.

1. Enjoy the 'Rise and Shine' meditation (page 16), taking the time just to be and to enjoy this new beginning. Feel happy to devote time to your Self. Set a clear intention for what you want to gain the most from this experience.

2. Explore the nature of your soul with the 'Me-within-Me' meditation (page 18), asking your inner being any questions that come into your awareness.

3. Call in your unicorn and Pegasian guides for a self-healing treatment. Don't set any intentions other than to simply be in the energy as it flows effortlessly through you.

4. Repeat the step above with a specific healing intention in mind.

5. Spend your *sadhana* in nature and enjoy the 'Awakening Your Senses' meditation (page 82), asking your unicorn guides to join you.

6. Invite in your unicorns and meditate together. Ask them to help you with your clairvoyance using the 'Developing Your

Clairvoyance' exercise (page 87) as your guide. If you have any fears around enjoying full spiritual sight, now is the time to ask the unicorns to transform these subconscious beliefs so you can move on with your life with a clearer perspective.

7. Repeat the step above but this time focus on advancing your clairaudience using the 'Developing your Clairaudience' exercise (page 90) as your guide.

8. Advance your clairsentience using the 'Developing Your Clairsentience' exercise (page 95) as your guide.

9. Advance your claircognizance using the 'Developing Your Claircognizance' exercise (page 98) as your guide.

10. Explore the many Source-led ways to start your day using the 'Rise with Purpose' exercise (page 108) as your guide.

11. Ask your soul to express your divine purpose in a way you clearly understand, for example by intuitively sensing and listening, by allowing your divinity to write, paint, sing or dance, or in any other creative way that comes to you.

12. Unicorns love to support you with creative visualizations that help the integration of your path, power and purpose. Invite them to join you and envisage a situation you'd like to create in your life. Bring as much detail and colour and as many positive vibes to this vision as you can. Let feelings of fulfilment flood your being as you see everything manifest in perfect divine order. Let this joy radiate through you, filling your space, then expand it out into your community, then into the world, and then imagine the whole universe being blessed by your joy. Bask in the knowing that Source is supporting the manifestation of your dreams.

13. Vision boards help to manifest the more physical aspects of desires, so create a vision board with your guides, gathering images that depict the situations you want to create in your ~~life. Hang your vision board where you'll see it each day and~~ trust your creations are coming to life.

14. Create a vision board for how you'd like to see the world, asking the *Sidhe* and the nature spirits to help you to bring the highest blessings to Gaia.

15. To amplify the vibrational frequency of your non-physical desires, write a list of the 'I AM' statements that are meaningful to you, such as 'I AM confident in all situations.' Place your list where you'll see it each day and read aloud what you're creating on a daily basis.

16. Enjoy 'The Marriage of Divine Love' exercise (page 146) to strengthen the relationship you have with your most significant other.

17. Connect with your spirit team to send forgiveness to a past experience for its highest healing and transformation.

18. Connect with your spirit team to send positive energy to a future event when you feel you could do with an extra Source boost!

19. Connect with unicorns and Pegasians to send Love to an aspect of Mother Earth or a planetary cause you feel passionate about.

20. Set up a devotional unicorn altar in your home to honour your guides and your soul, which is reflected by them. Because unicorns have a strong affinity with nature, you may wish to

decorate your altar with plants, flowers, crystals, shells or anything else that speaks to you from the natural world.

21. Create an altar in your garden to honour the nature spirits who support the land around your home. You may want to add the names of loved ones you'd like to enjoy greater laughter and abundance in their lives. Ask unicorns and faeries if they can support you in this cause. NB: Faeries appreciate little gifts you've made, especially something you've cooked with love – this can be placed on your altar as a token of appreciation for them.

22. Along with your unicorn guides, visit a silver birch or copper beech tree, asking the unicorns to support you in connecting to this tree, then the land, then sense yourself connected to the heart of Mother Earth. Journal what flows.

23. Have a unicorn shower! Before you turn on the water, ask your unicorn guides to infuse the water with their golden frequencies of fun, flow and prosperity. Soak up the brilliant goodness as it flows into your cells, activating your unicorn virtues from the inside out. You may also want to call on Pegasians to imbue the water with their rainbow frequencies. Be aware of the positive shifts that take place in your day as a result.

24. Along with your soul and spirit guides, write down what your core values are. What's most important to you? Are you living by these values? If not, what needs to change?

25. Along with your soul and spirit guides, write down what you appreciate about yourself. What aspects of yourself do you value? Are you allowing these aspects to be expressed freely in your life? If not, what needs to change?

26. Devote your *sadhana* to clearing out old beliefs using the 'Mental Spring-Cleaning' exercise (page 164) as your guide.

27. Recite the 'Me-within-Me' affirmation that's connected to the Prosperity Mantra (page 114) for 11 minutes, opening to the bliss that comes through to you from this mantra.

28. Create a song with your unicorn guides, enjoying the way they can help you to express your voice and unique Truth. Then dance to this song, asking your entire spirit team to join you!

29. In meditation, ask your unicorn and Pegasian guides to take you on a soul adventure, perhaps to the cities of Light they originate from.

30. Celebrate completing your 30-day consecutive journey. What have you enjoyed the most from this experience? What's your next soul adventure with your unicorn and rainbow team?

◊   ◊   ◊   ◊

Write Down Your Experiences

I recommend you write down your experiences of your daily soul-play in your journal. From repeating this programme many times, I can assure you that connecting with your soul and spirit team over 30 days, especially in the early hours of the morning when the rest of the world still sleeps, will bring you profound insights.

In recording what happens each day, note what your personal and collective intentions were, how your experience matched them and what happened during the rest of your day as a result of your *sadhana*. As your journey evolves over the weeks, you may want to record any emerging themes, patterns and areas to pay attention to, including any changes occurring within you, within your relationships and within the world around you. Are your beliefs and behaviour transforming and if so, how?

As you track your development, take the time to celebrate the breakthroughs you have, to feel good about the insights you receive and to share them with others. The more you savour these moments, the more you make this practice a positive, loving habit.

Keep Up and You'll Be Kept Up

If the going gets tough during your 30-day journey (and beyond), lean into your physical and non-physical support groups. If you are consistent in your practice, even if some days you're just sitting in silence focusing on your breath, it will become a great source of strength for you and will help to bring balance to all areas of your life.

Celebrate where you are in your energy and awareness each day, trying not to change your experience but to let it unfold naturally, for then your Truth can flow.

And if you're not sensing a deep connection with your unicorn guides at any time, go into nature and imagine your etheric horns are fully switched on and are radiating Light as you walk the Earth. Let your eyes, heart and soul adjust to witnessing the magic, joy and beauty of the natural world and you'll steadily experience the world of Spirit, too.

Lastly, and most importantly, by appreciating your journey and being compassionate towards yourself, you'll better understand your Self and in turn you'll soar. And you'll keep on soaring as you become the embodiment of your Truth, living your magic and loving with your soul.

Afterword

As we come full circle together, it's my sincere hope that you've enjoyed all the Love that's come from the unicorns and from my uni-heart to yours. If you've read this far without doing any of the attunements, exercises, meditations or #RisingReflections, please go back to the start and enjoy them in sequence – you'll be so happy you did, trust me! Plus, by the time you come to dive into your '30-Day Soul-Play', you'll be feeling squeaky clean from the inside out and prepared for the profound transformation that the next 30 days will give you. Be sure to join the online unicorn tribe too, for this is an adventure best enjoyed together.

The aim of *Unicorn Rising* has been to ignite ways of embodying your divinity in harmony with your humanity. No small feat! But the reward for choosing this path is as Infinite as you are, my friend. Throughout the book, you may have felt its vibration (and your own) steadily increasing. That was the unicorns' primary intention, so that as you personify your soul, you merge with the unicorn teachings and virtues, and evolve into the hero of your own story, learning/unlearning what you need to create your best life and ascend without doubts, fears or limitations. For you were born with greatness within you and now it's time to drop the excuses and be free, flowing where your heart wants to go and sharing your Truth with a world that's more than ready to see you shine.

For too long, I rejected this freedom. I feared change and the responsibility of being my whole Self. My guides had always said I'd be an author, but it wasn't until after Eden was born that I followed my intuitive guidance to sign up to a writer's workshop. Divine synchronicity and many signs from unicorns and Pegasians reinforced that this was the right way forward. Sitting in the train station after the course, I couldn't help smiling at how everything just works out for our highest wellbeing when we learn to trust when to ebb and when to flow in life. My joy must have been magnetic, as a little girl approached me and started to spin gleefully in a circle. The Light coming from her was so beautiful and it reminded me of how I'd spin in circles as a young girl, too. Just like a unicorn horn spiralling to and from Creation! That was when the concept of *Unicorn Rising* came to me in a flash. It was such a surreal experience.

And so here I am, beautiful soul, living my dream in order to reflect how much *you* can live *yours* too. Stay receptive to the opportunities that will enable you to display your gifts and make your contribution to the world and you will be on your way! Although there may be moments of mental interference after achieving what's important to you (as I well know), your soul and guides will remind you of your greatness and focus you on the next step. For example, despite my ego bringing in a new set of fears on learning of my book deal, I could hear my soul saying, '*Next!*' It was already focusing on a book tour, new courses, the next book and so on. Our soul never doubts our worth for a second or our ability to create an extraordinary existence.

As I come to closing this, my debut book, my physical act of shining my Truth and sharing my magic with the world, I have such appreciation in my heart. I'm just days away from marrying my best friend, centred in a realm of self-acceptance I couldn't have reached without the support of my unicorn team, and surrounded by the warmth of soul family members with whom I've reconnected through the Unicorn Healing® programme, many of whom have travelled across Mother Earth to be here for our wedding. As divine synchronicity would have it, these beautiful souls are here just as I finish this book, which they originally asked for! I hope you can feel my all-encompassing joy as I give you unending thanks for being part of this book, too, and its continued evolution.

If you'd like to continue your unicorn adventure and become a Unicorn Healing® practitioner, please visit www.calistaascension.com/UnicornHealing.

Until then, beautiful soul, may the Love that weaves us together continue to rise and shine as we co-create a brighter, more magical world.

And so it is. And so it is. And so it is.

Bibliography

Yogi Bhajan, *The Aquarian Teacher*™, The Kundalini Research Institute, 2003

Diana Cooper, *The Wonder of Unicorns*, Findhorn Press, 2008

Charlotte D'Aigle, *The Unicorn Dialogues: Encounters with a Magical, Mystical Creature*, Galahad Publications, 2013

Alice Fisher, 'Why the Unicorn has become the Emblem for our Times', *The Guardian*, 15 October 2017

Hugh Gilbert, *Free the Unicorn*, The Larry Czerwonka Company, 2013

Hilary Jane Hargreaves, *Walking with Archangels*, Unity Consciousness Books, 2017

Margaret Merrison, *What are Unicorns?*, Lulu, 2013

Adela Simons, *A Unicorn in your Living Room*, Matador, 2014

Baird T. Spalding, *Life and Teaching of the Masters of the Far East*, vols 1–6, De Vorss & Co., 1999

Jane Struthers, *Unicorns: An Introduction*, Summersdale Publishers, 2010

Acknowledgements

So many people have helped to create *Unicorn Rising*, it really has been a family affair! Unending thanks to my soul sis'star, Marie-Joe Fourzali, who created the illustrations. Your talent is as boundless as your Love and vision in bringing unicorn magic to physical life. Thank you for being so present and open-hearted in all you have shared and reflected – you're deeply loved. And to our extended unicorn family – the rainbow souls of the Unicorn Healing® programme – thank you for the asking for this book and for your continued support in its creation. I love how we can laugh, inspire and care for each other on our journey back Home.

Thank you, Mer and Per, aka Dawn-Marie Hanrahan and Ken Quinn, for your eagle-eyed proofreading and inspired suggestions. Your friendship means the world to me and I thank you with all my being for consistently seeing the best in this book and in me. Everyone needs a Mer and Per in their life!

Likewise, Nicola Hardman, Joumana Massoud and Cheryl Fryers – thank you, sis'stars, for never doubting the creation of this book, and for your giggles and adventures along the way!

To my local friends and those from afar in my social media communities, thank *you*! I am truly blessed to have you in my life and I appreciate you sticking around while I've been in writing hibernation!

Thank you to all at Hay House, especially Michelle Pilley and Amy Kiberd, for believing in the blessing of this book. And to my writer friends at the Hay House Writer's Workshop 2016, thank you for all your encouragement, and for the divine co-creations we've had and will have together.

To my unicorn guides, Hethgar and Princess, what to say that hasn't been said 1,000 times over?! You're a pure Source of inspiration and you've been there no matter what, holding space, always trusting, always faithful, always loving. And to the extended 'uni team' – to the Pegasians, dragons, angels, elementals, Elohim, Mother Nature, Father Sky and the Love of Source weaved within and without – thank you. I am here because of you. Thank you for guiding me to meet and merge with my soul and inspire others to do the same, and for carrying me at my lowest and cheering with me at my highest. What an adventure this 'living workshop' of life is!

And lastly, a deep bow to my mum, gran and all my ancestors for holding such sacred space. And to my best friend and, by the time this book is published, my husband, Greg, and our three rainbow boys, Eden, Rowan and Jack. Thank you for giving me the space to bring another baby into this world. Your warmth, giggles and home-made chocolate cake have been my fuel! I love you all-ways.

Other Works by Calista

Audio Downloads

Unicorn Healing® Mediations
(available to download at https://www.hayhouse.
co.uk/products/audio/audio-downloads)

This audio download includes six sacred attunements
to help you meet your unicorn guide, receive unicorn
healing energy, strengthen relationships, manifest a
compatible twin flame, assist your ascension journey
and more.

Attunement and Meditation CDs/MP3s

Activating your Light-Body

Align to your Divine Self

Awaken to Atlantis

Become Self-Empowered

Connecting to your Inner Child

Discover your Other Lives

Embracing Oneness

Falling in Love with You

Ignite your Light

Into the Heart of Gaia

Journey of Awakening

Living in your Heart

Loving your Body

Meet your Dragon Guide

Meet the Elementals

Meet your Guardian Angel

Meet the Mermaids

Meet your Spirit Guide

Sacred Aura Breath

Soul Healing with your Unicorn

Valley of Abundance

Manuals

Unicorn Healing® Practitioner Manual, 2009

ABOUT THE AUTHOR

Kelly McIntyre Photography

Calista is a Scottish-born author, speaker and pioneer of ascension. She has dedicated her life to helping others rise and shine, and has inspired thousands of souls worldwide through teaching her therapy systems Unicorn Healing®, Angel Healing® and Atlantean Crystal Healing™.

Through navigating postnatal depression, disease and trauma, Calista has gained a remarkable understanding of what it takes to heal and love ourselves. She is passionate about helping people to thrive, and provides soul sessions and workshops to cut through blocks quickly and gracefully, and enable profound shifts and a return to freedom.

From a young age, Calista has enjoyed a strong affinity with nature and elementals, and now shares her daily #MotherEarthNews on Instagram and regular Facebook Lives, imparting Earth-based spirituality and practical ascension tips.

Calista loves spending time with her boys and teaches Kundalini Yoga in her local community. She treasures family, friends and the little joys of life, believing the key to enlightenment is to honour our humanity as much as our divinity, while having as much fun as possible along the way!

For online courses and events, please visit:

www.calistaascension.com

◆ NOTES ◆

◈ NOTES ◈

◊ NOTES ◊

◇ NOTES ◇

◊ NOTES ◊